"Here is the next great conversion sto[...] immensely readable narrative. At once [...] overview, this is a must read for every li[...] Catholic who needs to remember the beauty of their faith, and every curious seeker wondering what is so special about the Church."

— PATRICK LENCIONI, *New York Times* best-selling business author and co-founder of The Amazing Parish movement

"I have been privileged to hear countless conversion stories over the past couple of decades. Kevin Lowry has been a friend throughout this time period, and I have seen God's grace transform his life over the years, little by little. I pray this book will encourage many people to say yes to Jesus, overcome hurdles in their own lives, and embrace the fullness of the Catholic Church."

— MARCUS GRODI, president and founder of The Coming Home Network International and host of EWTN's *The Journey Home*

"Conversion is not just for some folks, and it's not just for once. It's for everybody, and it's the ordinary way of Christian life. This book should be the last word of every RCIA program — and the starting point for every parish adult-education program."

— MIKE AQUILINA, author and EWTN host

"Let's face it, all of us at one time or another have been challenged by someone who disagreed with Church teaching. Maybe we've even been challenged by our own doubts or questions. That's why Kevin's book is such a great resource. It's an inspiring, practical, and extremely helpful tool not only for those considering coming into the Catholic Church but for cradle Catholics who need some encouragement as well as a refresher course in basic tenets of the faith."

— TERESA TOMEO, media expert, motivational speaker, best-selling author, and syndicated Catholic talk show host of *Catholic Connection* and *The Catholic View for Women*

"Every snowflake is unique and exquisitely beautiful, as is every conversion story; no two are alike. There is nothing like a good conversion story to inspire us, confirm our faith, and give us a good shot of spiritual adrenaline. Kevin Lowry has given us just such an inspiration with his new book, *How God Hauled Me Kicking and Screaming Into the Catholic Church*. Having converted to the Catholic Church myself twenty years ago, I can heartily agree with its title. Read his story, and wrestle with him through the eight stumbling blocks. You will be the stronger for it."

— STEVE RAY, author of *Crossing the Tiber*, producer of *The Footprints of God* DVD series and leader of Catholic pilgrimages (www.CatholicConvert.com)

"Kevin Lowry offers a beautiful gift to all Catholics and those considering the Catholic faith. From start to finish, his story of conversion is laced with humility, candor, and countless moments of God's grace. Kevin rightly shares that the flames of true conversion are always present in our lives: 'Conversion may flare up and then fade away again, seemingly to nothing, but the truth is that once it has taken hold it can never again become nothing.' I strongly recommend this book for anyone looking to be inspired and encouraged about our Catholic faith, and I also recommend it for anyone looking for an example of an authentic journey into the Church that Christ founded."

— RANDY HAIN, author of *Journey to Heaven: A Road Map for Catholic Men* and *Special Children, Blessed Fathers: Encouragement for Fathers of Children with Special Needs*

"Kevin has a beautiful gift of explaining how 'we don't know what we don't know.' Pick up this book and discover the Catholic world you've been longing for all along!"

— TOM PETERSON, TV host, author, speaker, and founder of Catholics Come Home

"A delightful mix of conversion story and apologetics, this book will help Protestants who are curious or on the threshold of the Catholic Church, as well as cradle Catholics who are looking for a refreshing, unique take on conversion, transformation, and the basic tenets of our faith."

— THERESA ALETHEIA NOBLE, F.S.P., author of *The Prodigal You Love: Inviting Loved Ones Back to the Church*

"Conversion necessarily involves a process of discovery. While this is usually uncomfortable, especially at first, we soon find that the Holy Spirit uses these discoveries — and even our discomfort — to order every aspect of our lives towards God. In *How God Hauled Me Kicking and Screaming Into the Catholic Church*, Kevin Lowry invites us all to embrace the divine drama that plays out in our everyday lives and to allow ourselves to be transformed through Jesus Christ and His Church. Read this book, and be encouraged to open your heart wide to the Lord's transformative love."

— DAN BURKE, founder of the Avila Institute for Spiritual Formation and SpiritualDirection.com, and executive director of EWTN's *National Catholic Register*

"Kevin Lowry hits the nail on the head with heart, humor, and holiness, sharing the raucous story of his circuitous route to the doors of the Catholic Church, opening them wide to those who might wonder what lies inside, and reminding those of us already in the nave of what a wondrous, joyous ship it is that carries us forward, with God, and not us, at the helm. Read *How God Hauled Me Kicking and Screaming Into the Catholic Church*, let it transform you through the grace of God, and brace yourself and your family for the glorious changes ahead."

— KEVIN VOST, PSY.D., author of *From Atheism to Catholicism* and *The Hounds of the Lord*

"*How God Hauled Me Kicking and Screaming Into the Catholic Church* by Kevin Lowry is a delightful read. With humor, grace, and charming anecdotes, the author bares his soul to demonstrate that faith is a fascinating adventure which continually transforms us. The author allays our fears, skillfully guiding us through all kinds of possible stumbling blocks to conversion. I highly recommend this book for converts, reverts, and cradle Catholics!"

— DONNA-MARIE COOPER O'BOYLE, EWTN TV host, speaker, and best-selling author of twenty books including *The Kiss of Jesus* (www.donnacooperoboyle.com)

"Kevin Lowry radiates joy. The man is simply a pleasure to read, in no small part because he embraces the fact that, in the words of the old adage, 'You shall know the truth, and the truth will make you odd.' He revels in the foolishness of the Gospel and gives us a story of his entry into its fullness that is winsome and delightful."

— MARK P. SHEA, author of *By What Authority? An Evangelical Discovers Catholic Tradition*

"I loved reading Kevin Lowry's new book, *How God Hauled Me Kicking and Screaming Into the Catholic Church*. Lowry winsomely describes his own unlikely conversion, illuminated by keen insights he's found by looking back on his life a few decades later. He combines an intriguing personal story with the foundational doctrines that every Protestant considering Catholicism must wrestle with. A winning combination."

— DEVIN ROSE, author of *The Protestant's Dilemma*

"What Kevin Lowry has crafted in *How God Hauled Me Kicking and Screaming Into the Catholic Church* is a book to guide you and challenge you on your journey to holiness. After you read it, you'll be compelled to take action in your own life so that your own conversion will continue. Thanks, Kevin, for a book that makes conversion more than just someone else's story."

— SARAH REINHARD, author and blogger (SnoringScholar.com)

"In *How God Hauled Me Kicking and Screaming Into the Catholic Church*, Kevin shares — with humor, humility, and brilliant insight — the stories of God working in his life. When you finish this book, I have no doubt that you will find yourself not just challenged but empowered to open your heart wide to God's transformative grace and the fullness of the Christian faith."

— SHANE KAPLER, author of *Through, With, and In Him: The Prayer Life of Jesus and How to Make It Our Own*

"To read *How God Hauled Me Kicking and Screaming Into the Catholic Church* is to experience the joy of the Gospel! No heavy tome of theology, no obtuse reflection on the interior life this. It is nonetheless theologically grounded and no less reflective of the joy-filled, Holy Spirit-fueled struggle of allowing oneself to be transformed by grace. I found myself nodding in agreement, smiling, and sometimes laughing out loud as I saw similarities between my conversion to the Catholic faith and Kevin's story. Whether you are a 'cradle' Catholic, a convert to the Church, a non-Catholic Christian, a practitioner of another faith tradition, or have no faith tradition at all, I encourage you to read this book and, God willing, be transformed."

— BROTHER REX ANTHONY NORRIS, spiritual adviser to the Coming Home Network International

How God Hauled Me
Kicking and Screaming
Into the Catholic Church

HOW GOD HAULED ME
KICKING
AND
SCREAMING
INTO THE
CATHOLIC
CHURCH

KEVIN LOWRY

Our Sunday Visitor

www.osv.com
Our Sunday Visitor Publishing Division
Our Sunday Visitor, Inc.
Huntington, Indiana 46750

Our Sunday Visitor Publishing Division, Our Sunday Visitor, Inc., 200 Noll Plaza, Huntington, IN 46750; 1-800-348-2440

ISBN: 978-1-61278-840-1 (Inventory No. T1646)
eISBN: 978-1-61278-843-2
LCCN: 2016935310

Cover design: Lindsey Riesen
Cover art: Shutterstock

PRINTED IN THE UNITED STATES OF AMERICA

Dedicated to my parents,
Margaret and Douglas Lowry,
for the firm foundation they gave me in life;
to my beloved wife, Kathi,
who helps keep me on the right path;
and to all our children and grandchildren;
whose lives I pray are transformed through Christ.

CONTENTS

Foreword

By Scott Hahn

I've heard Kevin Lowry tell his conversion story, and he usually zeroes in on a particular moment, which is particularly memorable for me since I was a part of it.

Kevin was still a Protestant, and I had gained some fame and notoriety for my conversion from the same brand of Protestantism. Kevin was persuaded, as I had been, but he also faced the million-and-a-half fears and hesitations I had faced. I knew that the way out of that foggy swamp was not argument, because each side always had a plausible counter-argument — plausible at least to a fearful, wavering soul.

So I reached into my pocket and handed him my rosary — blessed by Pope John Paul II. I gave it to him and urged him to use it.

It had worked for me. And it worked for Kevin.

For him, for me, and for everyone on God's green earth, conversion is not the matter of a moment. Nor is it the product of an argument won or lost. It is literally a turning (from Latin *conversio*) of the soul away from things and toward God.

Some people say that, technically, Protestants don't "convert" to Catholicism because they already have a place in the Church by means of Baptism. That's true in the most semantically precise sense. But I would argue not for this increasingly narrow definition of conversion but rather a broader application.

We're all converts. Every one of us. Everyone who's ever darkened the doorway of a confessional is a convert. We walk into the box as if we have a crick in our neck; we're facing the wrong way. It's unnatural. It's uncomfortable. We strain to see the light. It affects our reading, our driving, our eye contact with people we love.

Through confession and absolution, we're set free. We get the anti-inflammatory that enables us to turn this way and that — and we use that freedom to turn toward God.

Kevin Lowry gets this. He knows that we're all converts, and that we're going to spend a lifetime turning and turning and turning, ever more toward God if we do it right.

I'm grateful for the day I turned for a moment away from my arguments and toward the Mother of God. I'm grateful for the movement of the Holy Spirit that prompted me to point the same way to Kevin. I'm grateful to Kevin for taking up the challenge — and then setting it down for his readers, who, I hope, will number in the millions.

Transformed: Lessons of a Grateful Convert

Here's something I believe: If Catholicism is true, then it should change us. In fact, it should change everything about us. Here's something else I believe: The Church actually *does* have the capacity to effect change and in a way that is unique to her. And while we're on the subject of things that I believe, here's another: The evidence for the Church's ability to change us is everywhere. Throughout the ages, countless individuals have seen their lives transformed through their Catholic faith. For those who choose Christ and His Church, a lifetime of adventure awaits. Not the kind of adventure we see in movies but rather one of faith, a faith that grows until it permeates every aspect of our being. As we embark on the adventure by placing our lives in the service of God and others, transformation inexorably follows — the kind of transformation we were meant for.

A lifetime journey into faith and faithfulness in the Catholic Church may sound daunting, and perhaps it is, but it is also overflowing with meaning. The ultimate goal of such a life is nothing less than total *conversion*, which is another name for the transformation of which we have already spoken. To undergo conversion is to undergo a change; and in some form, this change is necessary for all of us, whether we come from another religious tradition or from a family that has been Catholic since before the death of the last apostle. To undergo conversion is to become different, or perhaps it is more accurate to say that it is *to be made* different. It is the start of the process of becoming a saint, for that is the ultimate point of conversion and God's goal for each one of us.

Becoming a Catholic — entering the Catholic Church — is often dramatic and frequently involves trading in our worldview for something that can seem foreign. It's seldom linear, and can involve taking one step forward, and two (or three) steps back. In my case, the seeds of Christianity were planted during my Presbyterian childhood. I made a decision for Christ during my pre-teen years, backslid a good bit subsequently, went to a Catholic college, and after some trial and error (mostly error), finally wound up coming into the Catholic Church. I was a true convert, by the way, since I had never been baptized (odd but true). Only after my baptism did I stop and look around, winded and breathing hard, and realize that I wasn't at the finish line.

I was only at the starting gate. My transformation — my conversion — had just begun.

But it *had* begun.

I should probably tell you right up front that getting to the starting gate was not easy for me. My conversion was neither the most straightforward nor the quickest one on record. I was good at resisting change, and before I took the plunge I stood at the water's edge for a long, long time. But I finally jumped in, and I'm here to tell you that the water's beautiful. I've been a Catholic for more than twenty years now — practically half my life — and from what I can see, the Church is what she claims to be: the specific road that Christ gave us to walk as we approach Him.

I believe that becoming a Catholic has enabled me to make more progress in my journey toward God than any other single act could have done. Christ has changed me through His Church, and I am confident that He will not be done with me until I have become the person I was created to be.

But there are some hard facts that I have had to deal with along the way. One of them is that the process of transformation takes time and is not all fun and games. It starts deep in the soul, showing itself first as a restless and often uncomfortable drama of the interior life. Step by step you find yourself becoming more and more committed to seeing the adventure of faith through to its end. Eventually, the discomfort fades and the restlessness wanes. Yet the adventure continues. At times, it barely seems to inch forward, and at others it hurtles on at breakneck speed.

Once we have reached that moment of grace, the instant when everything becomes different, we can see for the first time that faithfulness is what we have been yearning for all along, often without knowing it. It is, after all, what we were made for, and for that reason it begins to heal the pain and divisions in our soul — in our self. It quiets our useless anxieties; it tempers our need to grasp at the pleasures of this world as a drowning man might grasp at a piece of driftwood. In short, it begins to put things in order.

That moment of grace is what we often call conversion. But, as I've already said, conversion can rarely be reduced to a moment. A decision to open our hearts to Christ is certainly the first step toward transformation, but only the first. It is the moment when we discover our true selves and recognize our true home, but we have not yet become our true selves nor have we entered that true home. How many of us can claim to be like St. Paul on the road to Damascus, transformed in a moment of blinding clarity — so utterly changed that our old name no longer suits us and we need a new one?

Conversion may flare up and then fade away again, seemingly to nothing, but the truth is that once it has taken hold, it can never again become nothing. It can, however, become hidden, growing slowly and invisibly in your soul in a place that you don't even know is there. Then, suddenly, conversion springs to life again in a way and with a force you could never anticipate, and then you're back on the adventure, the one you only thought had ended.

By God's grace, I was baptized at age twenty-five and entered the Catholic Church. That was the moment of my conversion. It's recorded on my baptismal certificate, and I can tell you not just the date but even the time of day. Yet my conversion is still going on, and I hope it will continue until my earthly life comes to an end. Back when I was twenty-five, I had no idea that conversion was a process that would have countless beginnings but no end, that it begins anew every day. That was something I was startled and disturbed to discover. It made me feel like a failure, as if I wasn't doing something right, something very important.

Since that time, I've grasped that I was not a failure but a human being. I have also grasped that the process of conversion — even for cradle Catholics — necessarily involves turning our hearts again and again toward Christ. It involves growing in our understanding and practice of the faith.

That's the good part. The bad part was that I also learned that my heart was unruly and not always in the mood to turn to Christ; that despite my baptism, my heart remained stubborn and determined to turn in any direction but the one in which I wanted it to turn. In other words, I learned that I was not only a human being but also a sinful human being, whose understanding is partial and confused, one for whom practice can become rote and distracted. At times, it can seem almost empty.

And this is one of the reasons that conversion must be ongoing, why the adventure that God has begun in me and in countless others — continues. We are backsliders — all of us. We must constantly recommit. We must hunt for what we have lost and relearn what we have learned over and over again. This is an adventure that involves real work!

Like all Catholics, I have been given the tools to build a life of sanctity. But what good are tools if they are not used? The sacraments strengthen and feed me. They are the primary way God supports me on my adventure. The deep reality that lies at the heart of the Eucharist pulls at me when I am tempted to turn away. That reality urges me to turn back when I *have* turned away. It calls to me when I *try* to turn away, until once again I pick up my cross and follow the One whom I have found but still seek. I return again and again to prayers that have become rote, and eventually I am given the grace to find in them the meaning that seemed lost. I return to the confessional to discard the things that separate me from God, and I am renewed.

I have tried to walk the road of conversion for many years now, and I like to think I've learned a few things. In this book, I hope to share some of that knowledge with you. Let me make it clear that I am deeply thankful for my Protestant upbringing. It was both a gift and an excellent foundation upon which to build. I also have great respect and affection for non-Catholic Christians. Having spent a lot of time on both sides of the Protestant/Catholic divide, I understand what it is that makes the Catholic Church seem foreign and even threatening to the non-Catholic. I know what the big hurdles are, from where the roadblocks are likely to come.

Converts bring their own set of challenges to the Church. Much like immigrants to a new country, we must take time to learn the language, become culturally aware, and grow sensitive to the nuances of the faith. The richness, depth, beauty, and history of Catholicism are all vast, and we have varying abilities to assimilate them, to adjust to a new way of life.

For the last twenty years, I have been privileged to be associated with the Coming Home Network International. If you've ever watched *The Journey Home* television program on EWTN, you know something about the Coming Home Network. It was founded by Marcus Grodi — himself a convert, and a former Presbyterian minister. On his television program, Marcus has interviewed hundreds of converts and reverts about their journeys into the Church. As you might imagine, the stories are as diverse as the people, and I have learned a lot from them.

I want to share some of those insights. I hope this book will be helpful for converts, reverts, and cradle Catholics in whatever stage of the adventure they've reached. It is my greatest hope that it will also be read by RCIA groups and new Catholics. I especially hope that non-Catholics who are just beginning the adventure will take a look, for they are the ones who often stand outside the Catholic Church, yearning for a glimpse inside but unwilling to walk up to the door. I was once such a person, and I can vividly recall how strange the Catholic Church seemed, how off-putting it looked. Yet I can also recall the pull it exerted on me. I hope to speak to the person who is feeling that pull but still standing outside the door — or across the street or even down the block — and I want to let him know that his fears can be overcome, that her worries can be addressed.

So let's begin. First let me tell you a little about myself and how talented I was at avoiding becoming a Catholic. Then we can have a look at the things that helped me on my journey into the Church. I hope they'll help you, as well.

PART I

SPRINTING TO THE STARTING GATE

or

How God Hauled Me Kicking
and Screaming into the Catholic Church
Despite My Best Efforts to Avoid It

Chapter 1

Happy Easter! Now What?

Peter [said] to them, "Repent and be baptized, every one of you, in the name of Jesus Christ for the forgiveness of your sins; and you will receive the gift of the holy Spirit."
— Acts 2:38

I remember that night vividly, and I know I always will. My heart was pounding with excitement: I believed — hoped, prayed — that I had finally come to the end of a long and complicated journey, one that had led me to the last place I ever expected to find myself, leaning awkwardly over a baptismal font in — of all places — a Catholic church.

But had I really arrived? Had I truly come to the destination that God had in mind for me? I have to admit that even at that moment of no return, I was still having a little trouble accepting my own decision. This *had* to be the right choice, I reassured myself as I stood there; it simply had to be, because I was betting everything on it. By my side was my wife, Kathi, her presence a minor miracle. Up until that very night I hadn't known if she would be received into the Church with me, but here she was, and I was overjoyed. As I half stood, half crouched there, feeling rather foolish and working hard to bend my six-foot-four-inch frame into positions it was never made for, I could feel the warmth of her love and support. I can't describe how important that was to me.

But it was not her love alone that I felt. Toward the front of the church sat my mother and Presbyterian minister father, holding our two infant sons. I stole a surreptitious glance at them and smiled a smile I hoped they noticed. I waited, feeling my parents' improbable support as a source of tremendous comfort. In the midst of my lingering doubts, my uncertainty, I knew I had their blessing, and that meant a lot.

And I felt yet another kind of warmth as I waited that long-ago night, one that astonished and gratified me at the time. On my first visit to the church that was to become the place of my baptism, things had not gone very well. I had felt unwelcome, unnoticed, even invisible. No one had greeted me, or even acknowledged my presence. Catholics had still seemed a strange breed to me back then, cold and off-putting, unconcerned with the people around them — unconcerned (not to put too fine a point on it) with *me*. When had that all changed? And how had it changed without my quite noticing it? By the night of my baptism, everything had become different. It was as if I were surrounded by family, a family that actually cared — a family *I* actually cared about. Yes, it was the right decision, I told myself again, and this time I think I really believed it.

Then, finally, the cold waters of Baptism flowed over my forehead, and I was overwhelmed by a sense of mercy. It all seemed so simple — almost too simple. I was all too aware of my many years of sinfulness. I had regrets. In fact, I had loads of them. Were they all truly washed away by such a little bit of water, I wondered? If so, that changed *everything* — and I was born again at the age of twenty-five. I was new again. I was newer than my young sons.

And now, more than two decades later, I am deeply aware that it really did change everything. As I look back on the night when I became a newborn for the second time in my life, I recognize that a new world opened for me, or perhaps the world simply opened in a different way, enabling me to discern what had been there all along but which I had been unable to see — miracles that I had walked past like a blind man. Whatever the case, I was given something for which I had unknowingly yearned for most of my life: a sacramental world, a world that was simply suffused with God, a world in which holiness could be touched.

I was given tools that night to build a life of sanctity — tools I had never had before. I was offered new perspectives, new insights into human life, particularly regarding suffering and hardship — things that all those many years ago I didn't even know I would need. The waters of Baptism may have been cold that night, but through those waters I entered a relationship with Christ that was far deeper and far warmer than any I *could* have imagined otherwise.

By the way, my doubts, my uncertainty, disappeared a long time ago. I don't know exactly when. They just faded away over time until one day I realized that they were simply gone and I knew for certain that I really had found the place God wanted me to be. The Catholic Church is my home, and I have never thought about leaving it. In fact, after all this time, I don't think I could ever leave it.

Chapter 2

An Event *and* a Process

*May the Lord direct your hearts to the love of God
and to the endurance of Christ.*
                                — 2 Thessalonians 3:5

My baptism took no more than five minutes, but the journey
to the baptismal font took the better part of ten years — or
maybe I should say twenty-five years. In the beginning —
and the beginning lasted for a long time — I wasn't even
aware that a journey was underway, but it was, and God
was directing me down strange and sometimes uncomfortable paths, usually in ways I didn't even notice. Along those
paths, there were countless obstacles, humiliations, misun-
derstandings, and even estranged relationships. Yet they
were somehow all a part of that journey, all leading me, all
nudging me in one direction.

SLOW START

When did it really begin in earnest? It's hard to say, but I
usually date it to the time I was sixteen and exasperating
everyone.

Looking back at my life, I can finally see something that completely escaped my notice when I was in
my teens, but it was something my parents (and probably
everybody else) saw all too clearly: *something* needed to
be done with me.

To put it mildly, I was as cocky as they come. Since the time I'd been a small child, I'd been considered gifted; by the time I was sixteen, I thought that meant I was extraordinary. Not only that, I was running amok in the manner of many teenage boys: having a good time, not caring about (or even believing in) the future, driving everyone crazy with my world-class self-centeredness and devil-may-care approach to life. I was within a few months of graduating high school but had no inkling concerning what I would do next. For some reason that didn't bother me much: I was living for the day, for the moment, for the second, and the world was full of fun and overflowing with possibilities.

Out of all those many possibilities that stretched before me, however, there was one that did not occur to me. In fact it would *never* have occurred to me if I had been left to my own devices. Yet it was that very possibility that was to change my life, and it was offered to me one fine day by my dad, who, as I mentioned, was a Presbyterian minister.

He almost casually suggested that I take a few days off from school, which was just the sort of proposal guaranteed to capture my attention. Let me tell you, I lost no time in informing him that as far as I was concerned, he had come up with an excellent — perhaps even spectacular — idea. I was all ears when he told me he was contemplating a trip that just he and I would make: it was to be a road trip (great!) of international character (even better!). We would leave our native Ontario and drive south to the exotic and unknown (at least to me) land of Ohio. Why Ohio, you might ask (and, of course I did). Well, that was because Ohio was where a small university was located; it was a school my dad thought I might consider attending. "Terrific," I said, imagining beautiful college girls with flowing blond hair, "Let's go!"

At some point in the conversation (perhaps when I was emptying my sock drawer into my suitcase), he mentioned that it was a Catholic university, and that sort of startled my Protestant sensibilities a bit. I think I must have given him a quizzical look (maybe I even stopped dumping socks), but after my usual two-and-a-half seconds of deep analysis I decided I couldn't care less if the place was Zoroastrian, as long as I could have a few days off from school and take the promised road trip (and meet those girls with the flowing blond hair). Besides, I was just looking after all, not signing up for four long years. This was to be an adventure, not a commitment. And I was certainly up for an adventure.

ROAD TRIP

So we were soon on the road — my dad, me, some carefully folded maps (these being the days before GPS), and an absurd number of my socks. Our family station wagon was firmly pointed in a southerly direction, and I was still blissfully unaware that I was falling into a trap that my dad, my mom, and probably God had set for me. I hadn't a clue that my road trip would become more than a teenage boy's adventure, that it would irrevocably change the path of my life. All I saw was the possibility of having fun, of meeting new people. It never dawned on me to question why my father had chosen the school we were going to from all the possible schools in the world. I never even wondered very much why a Protestant clergyman was considering entrusting his son's education to a Catholic institution.

Religion, faith, the things of the soul, didn't show up on my radar screen very often back then. I'm a little embarrassed to say that even my parents' deep Christian faith didn't mean that much to me. Like most teenagers in our contemporary culture, I lived on the shiny surface of life, unconcerned with the possibility of any depth. I believed that God existed, and I had "accepted Jesus as my personal Lord and savior" in all sincerity during my pre-teen years (well … at least with all the sincerity of which a child that age is capable), but by the time I was sixteen, He had become remote — or perhaps I had. I had no trouble believing that God might be helpful in an emergency, but I had yet to encounter many real emergencies, so I usually kept God at a distance, out of sight and out of mind, like that fire extinguisher my parents had once bought, just on the off chance that it might be needed one day.

From Toronto we went through Buffalo, Erie, and finally on to Pittsburgh. Having received my license a couple of months before, I proudly shared the driving with my dad. As far as I was concerned, I was on the cusp of manhood, and with every passing mile I was feeling more and more collegiate. My time had come. I was on the move, and life was wide open before me, as wide open as the highways on which we traveled.

The drive lasted seven rather long hours, and I spent a lot of it committing everything I saw to memory. After we crossed the border, I found myself admiring the expensive and shiny new cars that so many Americans drove. I would have one of those someday, I decided, putting such a car on the rather extensive list of things I intended to acquire as I got older. As we drove on, however, I couldn't help but notice that not everything was shiny and new. The sleek cars were a stark contrast to the grimy industrial sections of the Rust Belt cities we were driving through. Even the odor of the air was different, I realized. As we neared our destination, it became particularly distinctive — filled with the smog of steel mills and coke plants.

We finally arrived in Steubenville, which was the name of the town in which the college we were to visit was located. As we did, the air seemed to become thick not just with smoke but also with desperation. I couldn't avoid noticing the poverty and living conditions. It was a dramatic change for me. I had never seen things like that in Toronto. I was in foreign territory, all right, and I wasn't sure I liked it. I vaguely considered mentioning the names of a few colleges in California to my dad. California — at least the California of my imagination — was all gleaming and new, and I was sure it would smell more like the sea than like soot.

The university itself turned out not to be the most spectacularly beautiful thing I had ever come across, but as my dad and I drove onto the campus it looked exciting to me. How could it not? It was going to be the scene of my adventure. The school, by the way, was called Franciscan University, and it was named after St. Francis of Assisi. Despite my very Protestant upbringing, I knew a little about him (who didn't?): he was kind; he liked animals, especially the cute, cuddly ones; he had an affinity for birdbaths.

My dad and I were given a dorm room to share. We were given tours of the campus. We were given brochures and other reading material. The students in general were surprisingly kind and welcoming. They seemed to like me, and I was impressed with their obvious good taste. I saw a few crosses (different from the ones I was used to: these had a crucified Jesus hanging from them) and other Christian symbols. I noticed the chapel and thought it looked weird and not like a church is supposed to look, but that was about the only impression that the religious nature of the place made on me. I had other, more important things on my mind.

I was biding my time, you see, eager for my adventure to begin. And finally my moment came. My dad was otherwise occupied and would be for a while. Seizing the opportunity, I told him I was going for a walk and made my way up a hill past the weird chapel to the academic buildings. I tried to work up some interest in them but found I couldn't, as they were just dull, drab, three-story brick buildings, about as boring as it was possible for anything to be.

So I continued wandering, heading toward the center of the campus, soon finding myself in the J. C. Williams Student Center. Miracle of miracles, it housed a campus pub, and almost immediately this pub started to exert some strange gravitational pull on my body and maybe even my soul. It was clear that I was in the grip of a powerful force. Resistance was futile, so I had no choice but to let myself be drawn inside. There I discovered that the miracles continued: beer was on sale for a mere fifty cents! Yes, this must be the place for me after all, I realized in a vaguely revelatory moment. My father was a very wise man, and Catholics were obviously very practical people.

Thanks to my above average height and a fake ID (which my dad didn't know about), I soon had my first can of American beer. Every drop was indescribably terrible, but I discovered that with perseverance and quantity the taste slowly but steadily improved. I was soon having a good time — the good time I had come to Steubenville to have. Despite being only sixteen years old, I was being accepted by college students as an equal, and that filled me with pride. I was feeling happier and happier, and I was becoming louder and louder.

Then in my growing exuberance I suddenly stopped, beer in hand, transfixed by a maple leaf on an article of clothing not far away. At home, this would be a commonplace occurrence, but I was far from home, a universe away from Toronto. I was in Ohio, in the United States, at a school named after a Catholic saint who liked animals. Maple leafs were out of place here. As I expanded my slightly fuzzy focus, the face of a shaggy haired, unshaven young man came into view. He was older than I was but not by very much, and seeing his maple leaf T-shirt was like beholding an oasis in the desert. After all, I was an expatriate, an exile who had found a fellow countryman. I was overcome with emotion.

THANK YOU, SIR. MAY I HAVE ANOTHER?

Slightly buzzed extrovert that I was, I jumped up to introduce myself to the only other Canadian in Ohio — the only other one for miles around, perhaps the only other one in the whole state of Ohio. Mark was his name, and he came from Montreal. Within minutes we were swapping stories from north of the border … and drinking more beer. We would be friends for life; I could feel it. Much to my amazement I learned from him that there was yet another Canadian on campus — a member of Mark's fraternity who hailed from the Toronto area, just as I did. There were actually three of us! I had to meet him. We would become a triumvirate; we would go down in the history of this school.

And meet him I did, as Mark and I soon left the pub and made our way to a dorm where many of his Tau Kappa Epsilon fraternity brothers — the TKEs — lived with plentiful beer in their rooms. The rest of the evening was spent meeting — and drinking with — the other brothers in the fraternity and enjoying their generous hospitality. By the end of the night, I was completely blasted and completely certain that Franciscan University was the place for me. I was going to be a TKE, and who cared that the place was

Catholic? In fact, who even remembered? It was a place where I would be happy, and that was good enough for me.

My exuberance began to fade a little as, in the early hours of the morning, I made my way back to the dorm room I shared with my dad, weaving every inch of the way. I discovered as I walked that someone apparently had moved the dorm since I had left it hours before — moved it and put it very far away. But I got there somehow and, incredibly, managed not to wake my dad as I fell heavily half onto and half off of my bed.

If somebody had told me that I had taken a small, almost infinitesimal, step toward becoming a Catholic that day, I would have laughed out loud. But I had.

Chapter 3

A Fish Out of Water

And Jesus wept.
— John 11:35

The miracles that flowed from that day continued, and they were not limited to cheap and plentiful beer. The first miracle was that my father forgave me for getting rip-roaring drunk and going missing until the early hours of the morning. The second was that after an appropriate period of anxious waiting, I was accepted at Franciscan University. So, several months later, after my rather inauspicious first visit, my dad and I were back in Steubenville. This time our car was stuffed with just about everything I owned, and my head was stuffed with dreams of becoming a TKE — certainly not with those of becoming a Catholic. I was excited, raring to go.

The odd thing was that I somehow still didn't really comprehend the intensely Catholic nature of the place that I, who knew nothing but Protestantism, was about to enter. My father did, but he was playing his cards close to his vest. I was very aware that the school was Catholic, of course; I had actually seen Franciscan friars in their long medieval-looking habits and knotted white cords (what was up with that?) on our first visit. But I didn't really grasp that they weren't just some quaint Steubenville custom, like a mascot at a football game — that they meant business. That would come, of course, but not for a while.

I did have some concerns, however. The most important of these was that I wanted — needed — to be paired with a suitable roommate. The word "suitable," as I'm using it here, should be understood in the following way: No judgmental Catholics need apply. But since I assumed that all Catholics were by definition judgmental, I realized the pool of possible applicants in a place like Steubenville might be relatively small (maybe even minute).

I hardly knew anything about Catholics at that point — and not only that, I didn't even know I didn't know much about them. What I thought I knew was little more than a mixture of nonsense, prejudice, and misinformation. That, of course, did not stop me from having deep emotional and mostly negative opinions. As I look back, I sometimes wonder where those opinions came from — certainly not from my father, who was always warmly disposed toward Catholics; he even seemed to admire some of them. It didn't come from my mother either, one of the most gracious and charitable people on the planet. I even had a couple of close Catholic friends as a child, and I certainly had nothing against them.

Yet, like many Protestants, I felt a vague suspicion of all things Catholic without really being able to articulate why. It was as if you had to be wary of them, had to make sure they didn't get the upper hand and try to reinstitute the Inquisition when you weren't looking. What I thought I knew could probably be boiled down to this: Catholics, generically speaking, were a superstitious and backward-looking bunch who thought they knew everything and wanted to control everyone.

I imagined what my dorm room would look like if I had a Catholic roommate:

- Dark, illuminated only by the light of a few tiny votive candles burning dangerously on a wooden bureau that had been turned into a makeshift altar.
- Pictures of dour-looking saints glaring down at me accusingly from the wall.
- The mumbled sounds of repetitive prayers being recited endlessly, and at breakneck speed, while I tried desperately to get a decent night's sleep.
- Clouds of heavy, sweet-smelling incense choking me, doing permanent damage to my Protestant lungs, and frequently setting off smoke alarms.

No, none of that was for me. I was a pro-active kind of guy, so I was going to do everything I could to make sure I didn't have to room with one of them. I wrote a lengthy and impassioned plea to the housing department at the school, explaining to them in great detail exactly what my roommate needs consisted of.

THE PROTESTANT ISLAND

Well, it worked, because I didn't get a Catholic roommate after all. I was assigned to a room with a sophomore who was the son of an Episcopal clergyman. Jon was an easygoing guy, exactly the sort I had hoped for — and not only that, he was a TKE, proving that the people in the housing office really knew their business. I was proud of the results my requests/demands had produced. I guess it never occurred to me that assigning the sons of Protestant clergymen to room together might have seemed a logical thing to do even without my expert guidance.

While I considered Jon as close to the perfect room-mate as anyone has a right to expect, I don't know how suitable Jon's father thought *I* was as a roommate for his son. When he and his dad arrived, luggage in hand, I was busily hanging up posters of rock bands on (what I had already claimed as) my side of the room. Outwardly, his father was kind, but I couldn't help but notice the way he rolled his eyes when he caught sight of my Led Zeppelin poster.

Nevertheless, the arrangement with Jon worked well. Our room was a small non-Catholic enclave, an island of rationalism in a sea of superstition. Not only that, it was filled with high spirits, great expectations, and enough beer to keep afloat any party that might unexpectedly spring into existence (which they often did through a peculiar kind of spontaneous generation that can occur only on college campuses). We shared an enthusiasm for the social — if not the religious — aspects of university life. We talked about everything and nothing.

To this day I recall our slightly slurred conversations, the goal of which was to attempt to calculate how much beer we could buy if we were to sell all the contents of our dorm room. After a certain amount of discussion, we decided that we probably shouldn't sell quite everything. We should keep a change of clothes each: it wasn't all that cold in Steubenville, especially relative to Canada, but it could get chilly at times. Of course we would keep the fridge as well, as it was essential to the proper enjoyment of beer. Our friendship blossomed as many such friendships do. The college years are a unique time in a person's life, a time when strong and lasting bonds can be forged. It is a time overflowing with possibilities, a time when you think the world is about to be spread out at your feet.

Jon would regularly play the song "More Than a Feeling" by Boston in the morning as we prepared to seize the day. It became a familiar accompaniment to our routine, to the point that we still call it "The Morning Song" with great affection.

Despite our best efforts, however, the Catholic spirit of the school did occasionally penetrate the heavy defenses of our little Protestant utopia. One night early in my first term, I was coming back to the dorm (from the pub, of course). I bounded up the steps to my floor, my long legs taking them three at a time, but I stopped dead when I got there. In front of me was a priest in full Franciscan habit, and he was throwing water at all the doors, one after another! If there was a fire, that little amount of water wasn't going to be much help, I thought. I knew, of course, that there wasn't a fire, but didn't have a clue as what was going on. Was I supposed to do something in response to this bizarre activity? If so, what? Whatever it might be, I wasn't going to do it.

Making a mental note to buy an umbrella as soon as possible, I made a dash for my room, ducking and weaving in a kind of ridiculous attempt to avoid the drops of water being flung in all directions around me. I didn't want them to touch me, not because I didn't want to get wet but for some other reason, one I couldn't express — but it was strong, nonetheless. This was some Catholic mumbo jumbo; I was sure of it, and I refused to participate. Returning to the room as quickly as I could, I swooped low, managing to dodge a dousing just in the nick of time.

"What the hell is he doing?" I demanded of my roommate, as I slammed the door shut behind me. With an air of superiority, Jon was quick to explain it to me. "It's holy water," he said.

"Huh?" I responded.

"Holy water. You know. He's blessing the floor and all the rooms on it."

I nodded weakly, but I still wasn't sure what was going on. As a Presbyterian, the notion of using holy water to help sanctify spiritually needy college students just didn't register. I stared at my roommate blankly, vaguely wondering if he was a plant, a closet Catholic sent to trip me up. Even if I could have grasped what holy water was, I doubt that I would have thought it would help. But I didn't want it to touch me, and I found myself wondering why. I couldn't really come up with an answer that made sense.

The whole incident somehow made me feel out of place — or rather, it made me aware that on some level I had been feeling that way all along. It actually triggered a number of insecurities that I was working hard to ignore. Despite my outward determination, I was actually feeling uncomfortable in my new surroundings. Was there anything behind the courteous smiles that everyone seemed to give me? Was it apparent I was only sixteen — younger than everyone in my class? Would anyone care that I was of a different religion, from a different country? Would anyone care that I didn't really belong?

YOU TAKE THE HIGH ROAD, AND I'LL TAKE THE LOW ROAD

Unsurprisingly, I spent my first semester at Franciscan reveling in the social aspects of the school. When I write "the social aspects of the school," what I really mean is that I didn't miss a beer blast all term. I generally attended these gatherings with the TKEs, the fraternity I was absolutely determined to join, and I soaked in every minute and every beer I could. I probably wouldn't have admitted it at the time, but I did struggle with homesickness a little (after all, I was only sixteen).

Occasionally, a wave of something that felt strangely like loneliness would sweep over me. With it would come a sort of vague and formless wistfulness, a desire to be in my hometown again, to see my friends, to eat my favorite food (pizza subs from Mr. Sub, a wonderful Canadian chain), and to drink real Canadian beer. Sometimes it was the desire just to stand on Canadian soil for a moment again.

At these times, I also felt acutely aware that I was different from most of the people around me, that they had this "Catholic thing" that connected them, that bound them tightly together in a way that didn't exactly exclude me, but made me sometimes feel like I was on the boundary line, too far from the center of things (and the center of things is the place I always wanted to be).

It didn't bother me a lot, but I was aware of it from time to time. I was also very aware of how to combat it: activity, people, and noise — lots and lots of noise — constituted a sure cure for this. These were the factors that enabled me to embrace my new life as a Protestant college student in a veritable ocean of Catholicism with aplomb. These were the things that enabled me to be happy, to win the campus billiard championship (a shining accomplishment of my freshman year), to avoid thinking about my schoolwork, my future, the consequences of my actions.

And my schoolwork was not going as well as I knew my father would have liked. Actually, it wasn't even going as well as *I* would have liked, and my standards were conspicuously lower than my dad's. Much to my surprise and chagrin, I learned early on that the professors actually expected students to attend class, and this was something I often didn't do, my social life being overscheduled, and my hangovers being lengthy and time-consuming affairs.

I was kind of shocked at my own painfully mediocre academic performance, as I had been accustomed to succeeding at school without actually having to do much work. But the courses at Franciscan were harder than I was used to and passing required effort, at least most of the time, and I was just too scattered and distracted to manage that. As a result of all this I began to feel a growing sense of dread. Happily, this, too, could be fixed with the magic trinity of activity, people, and noise.

It wasn't just the academic aspect of my college life I was ignoring. Although I was swimming in an ocean of Catholicism, I never got wet. I refused to let the religious aspect of Franciscan University, as ubiquitous as it was, register on me. It was a kind of willful ignorance, I guess. Looking back many years later, I am amazed that I systematically missed the treasures of the faith that I have come to love, even though they were all around me. Other people grasped them, and still others were grasped by them, sometimes unexpectedly, but they didn't even touch me; how could they? I had decided they were invisible — nonexistent.

Even worse than that, in my youthful arrogance and position as a proud Protestant outsider, I sometimes enjoyed taking a contrarian view, and sometimes even a mocking tone, when it came to Catholic things, especially the ones I judged absurd or meaningless (which was just about everything).

A CONFUSED CONTRARIAN

Perhaps the most obnoxious display of my ignorance and arrogance occurred one very ordinary day when I walked into the cafeteria for lunch. A couple of students had set up a table at the entrance and were asking for signatures on a pro-life petition. Most of the students were happy to comply, so there was a cluster of people around the table, and as I glanced at the petition, I could see that the list of signatures had grown long.

On that particular day, I was a little hungover and didn't have much patience for such things. I was, in fact, determined to walk by the table as if it didn't exist. By now I had become proficient in dodging contact with the committed Catholics on campus, many of whom were there to embrace the charismatic renewal. (We who had come to college primarily to party called them "charismos," with great derision.) Well, I guess my cloak of invisibility was malfunctioning that day, because I only got a few feet into the room before I was subject to the gentle proddings of some of the student volunteers.

"I hope you'll sign our pro-life petition," one of them said, as they all smiled at me. And then I did it. I opened my mouth, and I actually said, "No way, but do you have any pro-choice ones?"

I don't know why I said it; I was probably just as shocked as the students surrounding me at that moment. I wasn't sure that I really meant it, as I didn't understand much about the issue at all, but these do-gooder Catholics were bugging me, and I wanted them to get off my back and leave me alone. Immediately, one of the students jumped up from the table, strode over to me, and stood right in front of me. She was a short teenage girl with dark hair and a furious look on her face. Before I could even think of anything to say, she slapped me across the face as hard as she could. "How dare you!" she said, and stormed out the door.

Utterly shocked and stinging both from the slap and the embarrassment of being publicly humiliated, I decided that the problem was hers. "Can you believe that %$!@?" I asked the friends I was with. "What's her problem?" With as much bravado as I could muster, I continued through the lunch line, sharing colorful language and increasingly disdainful diagnoses of this young woman's pathology with my friends.

However, the experience remained on my mind for some time, and it bothered me — and what I had said bothered me even more. The young woman later called to apologize — for slapping me, not for objecting to my obnoxious comment, as she made very clear. I felt mortified by my own thoughtless behavior, but wasn't ready to admit it. I accepted her apology and mumbled something about not being Catholic and having a different perspective on the issue. But the whole event kept coming back over and over again.

She had been like a warrior when she confronted me. Where did all that emotion come from? Where did that commitment come from? I couldn't figure it out, but the do-or-die passion of it all seemed almost enviable. I began to wonder if I could work up such passion for anything and found I couldn't answer the question. I didn't know what to do with what had happened, with the feelings that had been stirred up inside me. So I did what I always did: I put it aside and turned to the next pitcher of beer.

Chapter 4

Soused in Steubenville

Consider it all joy, my brothers, when you encounter various trials, for you know that the testing of your faith produces perseverance. And let perseverance be perfect, so that you may be perfect and complete, lacking in nothing.

— James 1:2-4

The next couple semesters did little to alter my opinion of Catholics. They did, however, do quite a lot to diminish my confidence and increase my anxiety.

I was sitting in the cafeteria one Sunday morning, wearing my hard-won TKE shirt. (Yes, they accepted me! I had become one of the chosen few! My goal had been achieved, but now what?) My mediocre breakfast consumed, I sipped a cup of strong coffee while doing my best to bask in my newfound freedom, a freedom that enabled me to (among other things) avoid attending church on a morning like this. Somehow, however, no matter how hard I tried, I couldn't quite summon up my customary self-satisfaction, my normal enthusiasm for life. Not only that, various concerns kept popping into my mind unbidden, and after a while my stomach began to churn in a way that was new to me. "It must be Steubenville's coffee, which is at least as bad as its beer," I told myself. Staring accusingly into the depths of my cup, I contemplated switching to tea.

What I needed, I decided, was something to take my mind off things — a diversion — but after a quick glance around the cafeteria, I realized I wasn't likely to find any worthwhile distraction there. The place was nearly empty, and the few people who were there looked more or less like I felt, which meant they were to be avoided.

Pushing my guilty coffee cup away from me, I glanced out the window, my gaze falling on the chapel for no reason other than that it was there. I realized that it seemed quiet, sort of peaceful, and I remember that feeling of peacefulness being strangely appealing to me on that long-ago Sunday morning. I, who tried so hard to fill every second of my life with activity, actually liked the stillness of that building outside the window. It certainly wasn't beautiful, but I liked looking at it. And then, without warning, the peace that I had found only a few seconds before was utterly shattered, as the doors to the chapel burst open and the races began. Students swarmed — flooded — out, and a stream of Catholic humanity rushed in my direction — or more accurately, in the direction of breakfast. Most of them were walking quickly, but in the front some actually began to run.

I grinned as I watched, feelings of Protestant superiority floating to the surface. Thoughts of my dad's church flashed through my mind. How different this was from the dignified services he led. Effortlessly, I brought to mind a thousand images of people standing around with my dad long after the last hymn had been sung. In the world from which I came, sharing leisurely conversation, gentle laughter, and fellowship was the norm after religious services, not mad dashes for food begun while the organist still had a verse or two to go. I wondered what the priest who had just celebrated Mass in the chapel felt like as he watched his congregation bolt away from him like a herd of horses in a stampede. These Catholics looked like they were running from Beelzebub himself! They had a lot to learn, I concluded rather smugly.

Oh! There it was: the sense of self-satisfaction that had been eluding me was back where it belonged.

HUNGER GAME

They got closer and closer until the front runners exploded through the cafeteria entrance, and I couldn't help but join in the scattered applause and cheers that greeted them. Despite their obvious embarrassment, the recent Mass-goers/current sprinters grabbed their trays and got in line for their dubious prize: rubbery scrambled eggs.

As more hungry students streamed through the doors, I was astonished to see two good friends in the midst of the crowd. I stood up and waved to them, but I don't think they noticed as they maneuvered themselves toward the food. Had they actually gone to Mass, I wondered, sinking back into my chair and feeling invisible. That didn't compute — we had all been at the same party the night before, and it had been pretty intense. With the shape they had been in, I was not just surprised that they hadn't slept the day away but that they could actually stand, let alone run. What was it that got them out of bed and into the chapel that morning — a tractor beam? I worked hard at solving this mystery as I sat there, so hard that I forgot that I had sworn off coffee only minutes before and swallowed a big, bitter, tepid gulp that made me grimace.

As the tables around me filled up with smiling and laughing students, the seeming happiness surrounding me proved not to be the distraction for which I yearned. In fact, it served only to accentuate my own sadness, brought on by my uncertain and rather precarious future. Despite straight

A's in what my father referred to as my "double major in beer and billiards," my academic grades were abysmal, and I was already on probation. Would I flunk out? It was a distinct possibility. What would I do if I had to leave? The thought of losing my treasured independence was too terrible to contemplate. Maybe I should have gone to church that day after all.

Perhaps it was the giddiness in the air, but as the noise levels rose, my spirits sank. Staring into my coffee cup — which seemed to have become my standard response to everything that morning — wasn't giving me any comfort, and it wasn't providing any answers either. Where was all the happiness coming from, I asked myself, almost angry at the people who surrounded me. And what were they giving out in that chapel? Whatever it was, it sure wasn't on the menu at the cafeteria.

THE BEGINNING OF THE END

The world seemed to be closing in on me. Feeling dejected, I got up slowly and shuffled toward the exit. I needed some time to think, and (unusual for me) I needed to be alone.

Trudging from the cafeteria and weighted down with a vastly-out-of-proportion sense of doom and gloom, I was only too aware that my predicament was largely self-inflicted. (Okay, it was *completely* self-inflicted, but back then I couldn't quite admit that, even to myself.) I was having problems — that much I could admit — and some of them were beginning to scare me. Just the week before, I had somehow managed to lose the memory of the better part of a night (something that didn't strike me as a good sign). I had been out late, drinking copious amounts of cheap beer with a few fraternity brothers. That part of the evening was clear enough, but what about the rest? No matter how much I struggled to recall, I simply couldn't. Various bits and pieces of memory occasionally rose to the surface of my consciousness and then faded away again, but that was about it. It all seemed vague, hazy, like a dream that somebody else had dreamt and only told me about.

Deciding the best course of action for me was to worry intensely as I walked, I let out a slightly dramatic sigh of frustration (I was in the process of becoming the lead character in a tragedy after all) and concentrated my thoughts on that stolen night and its aftermath.

The aftermath, by the way, had been somewhat embarrassing. Our dorm director, T.J., had approached me the morning after the missing night. "What time was that, anyway?" he had demanded, his normally affable voice loud, gruff, and angry. I had stared at him blankly for a moment, and then, doing some fast thinking, concluded from his question that we must have run into each other on the infamous night in question. A weak smile was about the only response I could manage, so I gave him one, hoping for further clues as to what I had said or what I had done (whose car I had stolen, who I had married). None, however, were forthcoming, as he apparently had the strange idea that I actually had a functioning memory. Still desperately hungover, I finally just threw up my hands and shook my head. I think I mumbled, "Sorry . . . really, really sorry," or something like that, as I sheepishly withdrew.

I found myself shaking my head once again as I walked across the campus. How could I have been so stupid? What was happening to me, and why were so many things going wrong all at the same time?

I shivered, realizing for the first time how cold it was outside. What was up? Normally, the fall weather in Ohio seemed balmy to me compared to Toronto. I took a deep breath of frigid, smoggy air but immediately regretted it. The unmistakable stench of the steel mills of Ohio filled my lungs, making me suddenly queasy. I shivered again and pulled my coat more tightly around myself, wondering if maybe the problem in the pit of my stomach wasn't wholly the fault of bad coffee. In fact, maybe it was something else entirely.

DOWNWARD SPIRAL

That's it, I realized, suddenly filled with hope: I was coming down with something! Maybe I was on the verge of being really, seriously sick with the flu — an exotic American strain of it for which my Canadian immune system had no antibodies and for which doctors had no cure. Even as I walked, my body was fighting a valiant but doomed battle against vast armies of aggressive viruses. I didn't stand a chance. I would have no option but to take a medical incomplete for the term — an incomplete that would solve (or at least postpone) all my problems. It was a gift from God: the gift of perfectly timed illness. Hallelujah! I.C.U. here I come!

Making a mental note to attend church next Sunday to express my gratitude (if my doctors didn't forbid it), I eagerly felt my forehead, expecting it to be warm ... hot ... burning up. Then I frowned and turned out of the wind to feel it again. No matter how much I tried to believe that it was warmer than it should be, I failed miserably. My joy was short lived; it looked like I would not be rescued by illness after all. Perhaps I wouldn't be rescued *at all*. I trudged on, desperately worried about what would happen if I didn't change my ways, and even more worried that it might be *too late* for me to change my ways.

Still trying to feel sick, I was unable to put the incident with the dorm director out of my mind. Since I had no direct knowledge of what had happened, I had had to piece it together from information supplied by others. It had been an awkward task, but I had been determined — it was a night out of my life after all, and I wanted to know what had gone on — so, by a couple of days later I was in possession of all (or at least most) of the relevant but embarrassing facts.

It seems that I had returned to the dorm way past 1:00 a.m., when the doors were locked by security. Whether I didn't have my keys or was too incapacitated to use them, I have no idea. But apparently one thing that I had understood in my inebriated state was that I needed to get into the dorm, so I began pounding on the nearest window and shouting loudly. It was the dorm director's window, as it happened.

My friend Jamie had been the one who finally helped me connect the dots. He actually seemed to enjoy regaling me (and far too many others) with the sordid details. His version was colorful and hopefully slightly hyperbolic. Jamie's room was above the dorm director's, and when he heard the ruckus (which, apparently, many people had) he had rushed downstairs, two steps at a time to find me swaying back and forth while getting chewed out by a tired and very grumpy T.J. "You were obliterated!" Jamie always thundered as his story reached a crescendo. Somehow he was able to make the word "obliterated" go on for a lot longer than most people could.

T.J. was generally a pretty amiable guy, but the whole event had really annoyed him — and it really embarrassed me. When he had chastised me, his tone had been no-nonsense (in fact, it was almost fierce), and I had thought I was in for real trouble. But when push had come to shove, he had taken the most lenient route possible and had only given me a strong warning, rather than referring me to the administration for disciplinary action. My sense of relief had been palpable — and it still was. I had escaped by the skin of my teeth. Why, I wondered, had he let me off the hook?

And then I realized that while my mind was firmly ensconced in the clouds, contemplating my reprehensible recent past, my body somehow had migrated to the chapel, not far from the door that had burst open, disgorging hungry students mere minutes before. I stopped to look at that door as a cold breeze blew by, and found myself wondering what lay beyond it. Then all was quiet for a while. The peace that I had imagined before slowly began to seem imaginable once again, but it was a peace that I couldn't touch, something close yet unobtainable (kind of like my memory).

I stood there examining the stucco walls, and after several minutes I decided the chapel didn't look so bad, although the exterior structure still bothered me, as it had since I had first seen it. It was so different from the rectangular churches I had always known. Part of the building was round, with the roof jutting upward toward the sky in the shape of a ship's sail toward the front, supporting a cross.

In my months at Steubenville, I somehow had never gone in — never even looked in. But that morning something was niggling at me: I wanted to know what it was that had drawn so many students so early on a day when they could have slept till noon. I looked toward the door and wondered if it would be locked. I tried to imagine how heavy the door would be if I tugged on it to open it. Would it be warm inside or cold, dark or light, ornate or austere?

The wind blew again, filling my nostrils with more industrial smog and feeling cold on my face. It ruffled my hair, reminding me that I needed a haircut. And then I realized that something — I don't know what — was different; something had come back to normal — to the way it should be, the way it always had been. I began to chuckle and to shake my head in mock horror. Whatever was in that chapel that looked like a ship's sail and spewed forth sprinting students on Sunday morning, I knew it hadn't anything to do with me. Many of my friends had survived their excursions into the chapel seemingly unscathed. But I did not belong there; I was an alien from a different world — a better, more rational world.

Besides, I reasoned, the building might spontaneously combust if I went inside. I knew enough of the Bible to know that God could send lightning strikes or cause natural disasters if He wasn't happy with people, and I was pretty sure He wasn't happy with me.

CAROL

So I never looked inside the chapel that day when I felt so sad. I walked away instead, without ever even touching the door. I would not enter it for a long time to come, but I thought about it sometimes, and I thought about the people who entered it to pray, to attend Mass, to do whatever it was that Catholics did in a church. I thought often of my roommate's girlfriend's devotion to that building. Her name was Carol, and I'm ashamed to say I gave her a hard time about her frequent chapel visits. For some reason, she and I would talk often about religion. Our conversations would almost always follow a distinct pattern, one set by me. This is the pattern:

> **Me:** "Why would anyone pray to Mary? You should only pray to God. And what about

kneeling in front of statues? That's not just weird — it's idolatry!" (As you can imagine, I didn't win any prizes for ecumenism back then.)

Carol: "No, it's not, Kevin. You don't understand. I don't pray to Mary in the way I pray to God. I ask for her prayers. I pray *through* Mary. Mary points us to Jesus. And, by the way, nobody prays to statues. The statue only represents the saint." (But Carol should probably have won a prize for not punching my lights out.)

Me: "Praying through Mary doesn't make any sense! I don't care if she points us to Jesus or not. We can go straight to Him!" (Not that I did that very often, mind you, but I knew you could if you wanted to. My father had told me so.)

I could go on, but I assume you get the idea.

I made it back to my dorm room that day in a depression so extravagant that it could only have been achieved by an adolescent. "Why me?" I asked again and again, convinced the entire universe was conspiring against me and hoping for some answer that was different from the all-too-obvious one.

But none came, and eventually I had to accept reality, had to accept that the strange feeling deep in my gut (which grew until it felt as if I had somehow swallowed a bowling ball) had nothing to do with Steubenville's bad coffee or a mutant strain of the flu. It was actually the weight of responsibility, something I had tried desperately to avoid for most of my life. Through a calculated negligence, the situation had come to rest on my shoulders, and I knew it. Worse yet, one of the things that bothered me most about the predicament was knowing that if I got kicked out, I would leave many dear friends behind. Friends like Jon and Carol … and numerous Catholic friends, oddly enough.

Chapter 5

Fast Forward

The Lord does not delay his promise, as some regard "delay," but he is patient with you, not wishing that any should perish but that all should come to repentance.

— 2 Peter 3:9

"Shut that *$&#~$^ thing off!" I shouted.

"Hey!" a sharp and disapproving voice from upstairs called out, startling me. I had thought my dad had left already. Obviously, he had not. Shamefaced, I went upstairs.

"Sorry about that, I ... guess I didn't know anyone was home."

My dad, looking none too pleased, was uncharacteristically direct. "Were you planning on going to church today?"

I gave him a blank look in response.

"Well, you are now."

And that was that.

I was trapped again. It had become a bad habit, and I sighed. (Sighing was becoming a habit too. In fact, by this time I had pretty much perfected my sigh; it was a flawless blend of world weariness, condescension, and stoicism — a sigh to be proud of.) My friend, Brian, by the way, who was visiting on that Sunday morning, was the one who caused the whole stupid mess and got me trapped. Now, like it or not, we had to go to church rather than spend the morning goofing off. Life is unjust. The good so frequently suffer.

Of course, I was being unfairly punished, as my profanity-laced command had actually averted a disaster. Everybody knows that running a microwave with nothing in it was something you shouldn't do — everybody but Brian, who thought that doing so as an experiment might be both fun and educational. The object of the experiment was to determine if the machine would melt itself. Whether it would or wouldn't have caused a meltdown in our kitchen, I knew that destroying the microwave would have caused a meltdown in my life. So I had simply told him that he needed to turn it off. The command was good — even laudable. It was my choice of words that did me in.

I would have to be more careful with that, I thought on my way to church. Obscenities seemed to do more damage to me than they were worth. During the sermon, I decided on a new goal: reforming my vocabulary.

NEW BEGINNINGS

If anyone's confused about the above anecdote, let me explain. It took place a couple of months after my morose and doom-laden walk across campus that I described in the last chapter, which means that it took place not long after I was rather unceremoniously asked to pack my bags and leave Franciscan University, Steubenville, Ohio, and the United States. I include it as a way of demonstrating that the abject failure of my adolescent rebellion and the ignominious termination of my college career didn't result in a spontaneous surge of maturity.

By the way, I left college in a blaze of glory, with a 0.549 GPA in my final semester. That takes effort. Not just anyone can manage something like that. I also include it to show that the vague desires for something deeper than the ordinary things of life — for God, actually — which were just being awakened in me at Steubenville, went into hibernation again. It was sort of like when those first brave, green shoots of new life emerge in the spring and are then quickly buried under a late snowfall.

So, just a couple of weeks shy of my eighteenth birthday, I found myself moving back into my parents' house, both my college career and scrupulous beer-drinking routine rudely interrupted. I was completely humiliated, and no other school would have me. I knew I had to do something with myself, and that meant I had to get a job. The problem was that I had no skills to speak of and therefore no prospects. I was pretty good at billiards, but that seemed to have limited advancement potential. As I said before, I was trapped.

Desperate to find a job — and willing to do just about anything to redeem myself in my dad's eyes, I plunged into a frantic search for employment. Within a month — although it seemed like an eternity — I was miraculously given an opportunity to work at Sony of Canada, Ltd., through one of my dad's friends. I started as a computer operator, solidly on the bottom rung of the corporate ladder. Although it bothered me to live at home, particularly after having breathed the (smoggy) air of freedom in college, the situation did come with certain advantages. Primary among them was that I had lots of discretionary income. My budget was simple but robust, containing categories for my sports car, food, entertainment, beer, and not much else. (Okay, so my beer drinking was only temporarily interrupted by leaving school. I had, however, developed a certain sense of moderation concerning it, as I actually wanted to remember the events of my life.) Things were looking up, and stung by my experience at Steubenville, I was fiercely determined not to fail this time.

Slowly but surely over the next three years, this determination actually led to real results. I began to develop a serious work ethic — something that surprised nobody more than me. As a direct result of that, I received a couple of promotions at work and got my first taste of success. It didn't take me long to realize two things: the first was that success tasted pretty good; the second was that I wanted more.

LOFTY GOALS

Lately, though, it was beginning to dawn on me that I needed to return to college in order for my career to reach the lofty heights to which I now aspired. After having worked in what was then called Management Information Systems (MIS) for over two years, I had transferred to the marketing department. It was a good move, since the MIS general manager (my dad's friend) and I did not hit it off. In my new role, I had the opportunity to work under Japanese and Canadian managers, who were smart, hardworking, and successful.

In addition to my job responsibilities, I volunteered to help out on the company's social committee. Given my youthful enthusiasm and boundless energy, I soon found myself "promoted" to president of the committee. Among the most unexpected benefits of this high office was that I was given the privilege of a personal meeting with the president of the company to outline our plan for the annual Christmas party and beg for a budget. I was thrilled. As the date for the meeting neared, I was bursting with nervous anticipation.

After what seemed like an eternity, the day of the meeting arrived. I was gratified to receive a warm welcome at the president's office. As I looked around, I was struck by the enormity of the place, which dwarfed my small cubicle and contained beautiful, ornate furniture, including a sofa that looked like it cost about as much as my car. The president was gracious, and we hit it off immediately. A busy man, he came straight to the point, approving a generous budget for the Christmas party.

Sensing that our meeting would not last long, I decided it was time to impress him. "I'm really grateful to work here," I blurted out, "but I'd like your job —." I stopped dead. My mouth hanging open, I just stared at him, realizing what my words must have sounded like and wondering how long he'd give me to pack my things. "Someday — I meant someday ... a long — a *very* long — time from now ... when I'm ... really ... old and you're ... dead — gone — retired, I mean...." I sputtered trying to fix things and realizing that words, even if they weren't obscenities, could still get you into trouble.

Well, I guess he didn't feel threatened, because with a chuckle and a smile, he thanked me for the committee's work and headed off to a meeting. I stood there for a moment, slightly dazed, replaying our brief conversation in my mind, and then the adrenaline seemed to drain out of my body. It was as if I had just met the prime minister, or Bono from U2. I had just shaken the hand of greatness. Despite my emotional exhaustion, I staggered back up the stairway and returned to my tiny cubicle, smiling the entire time and thanking God that I didn't have to pack up and leave.

My brief meeting with the president of Sony inspired me. I wanted to succeed as he had succeeded. But how could I do so without a college degree? Within Sony, all the big shots had degrees. In fact, many of them had MBAs. What I needed was an MBA too, and I decided to get one. There was just that minor matter of completing an undergraduate degree first.

SECOND CHANCES

As I sat daydreaming in my cubicle, my dad's influence was playing on my mind as well. I had started early and skipped a grade in school, but he had skipped two grades. He was hard to keep up with! After earning his undergraduate degree in history, he got a graduate degree in theology and was ordained a Presbyterian minister. He and my mom had been missionaries in Nigeria before dad applied for business programs. After topping his class in the first year of an MBA program at the University of Western Ontario, he was advised to stop messing around and get a doctorate. He did so, earning his Ph.D. in international business at MIT's Sloan School of Management.

I, on the other hand, was a college dropout organizing Christmas parties at Sony. I took a deep breath. Things were going well, especially now that I had achieved some level of success in the "real world." But despite my meeting with the president, and the fifty-million-dollar budget I oversaw in procurement at the time, I knew there had to be more to my future than selling loads of TVs — even if they were awesome TVs. Didn't there?

Over three years had passed since leaving Steubenville, and I was ready to redeem myself. In fact, I was more than ready to do what I couldn't do the first time: to buckle down and pursue my studies — to make something of myself. So, as the weeks wore on, I made a few tentative glances and then a few not-so-tentative glances in the general direction of institutions of higher learning in both Canada and the United States. Now, I'm basically an optimistic kind of guy, but let me tell you, the reaction I got didn't encourage me much. I learned very quickly that my brief but flamboyantly abysmal collegiate career was something like a criminal record that couldn't be expunged. In other words, three years of success at Sony did not seem to matter.

My nearly microscopic grade point average made me an outcast in the world of academe, an untouchable. This was getting me down, but one day, as I sat at my desk, an image of those students running from the chapel at Franciscan University popped into my mind. I found myself smiling, almost grinning at the memory, and then it occurred to me: Maybe — just maybe — Franciscan would give me a second chance. I lost no time in calling the admissions office. I had a plan, a last-ditch effort, and I had a strange feeling it was going to work.

DISTANT EARLY WARNING

What I didn't quite realize was that the tractor beam that brought my friends to Mass in that chapel at Franciscan was beginning to work on me now. I couldn't feel it yet; I couldn't feel much of anything but my own desires and ambitions. I still hardly gave a thought to God, to religion, to church of any kind. Despite all that, however, something was pulling me back toward Steubenville, toward a new life — toward New Life.

So, I won't bore you with too many details. Suffice it to say that I contacted Franciscan and initiated a certain back-and-forth dialogue that sometimes seemed promising and sometimes seemed discouraging. The upshot was that they were skeptical (I can't imagine why) but willing to consider me — perhaps out of Christian charity. It was, however, made abundantly clear to me that I would be on probation from day one, that the antics of my past would not be tolerated in my future. I was told that I would be given one semester to pull my cumulative grade point average up to a barely respectable 2.0. I didn't even have to do the math, but I knew that meant that I would have to achieve stellar grades to average with my nearly non-existent earlier ones or I would be on my way back to Toronto yet again.

I admit it sounded daunting, and a few years before I probably would have been scared off, but I took a deep breath and agreed. This time, I knew that I could make it work. I had to, as there were no other options, at least none that I could discern.

Don't worry. I won't keep you in suspense: I did it. I actually did it! I did it by the skin of my teeth, but that doesn't matter because I did it. After a rather grueling semester as a business major (a dramatic switch from my major during my first time at Steubenville, which was psychology) I pulled an almost miraculous 3.85 grade point average. When averaged with my earlier marks my new grades were enough to allow me to just squeak by. I had redeemed myself! I was ecstatic; my parents were elated; my friends were bewildered; my professors were stunned. All of that was important to me, but somehow it paled before the fact that Kathi was pleased.

Chapter 6

The Beautiful American

*You are beautiful in every way, my friend,
there is no flaw in you!*

— Song of Songs 4:7

"Who was Kathi?" you might wonder. Kathi was my destiny — or at least part of it. She is part of the reason God brought me back to Steubenville when I probably had no right to be there. She is the epitome — the archetype, the perfect example — of the beautiful American college girl with flowing blond hair that I yearned to meet on my first visit to Franciscan University. She was a nursing student when I met her and, wonder of wonders, a fellow Protestant. She is now my wife, the mother of our children — facts I thank God for every day of my life — and a devout Catholic. She is a unique joy in my life. And she is one of the main reasons that I worked like a maniac to make the grade point average that would keep me at Steubenville . . . that would keep me in her wonderful presence.

I first glimpsed Kathi across a crowded room. Yes, I know that's a terrible cliché, but it's true. I can't say that it was love at first sight, so I can at least avoid that cliché; and yet I can say that I had a feeling that, in seeing her, something important was happening to me — and I wanted a closer look. We exchanged a few words, nothing earth shattering, probably nothing that was even very interesting. I was uncharacteristically tongue-tied, something which may or may not have worked in my favor.

I decided I had to get to know her; in fact, getting to know her became a rather consuming goal in my life. Unfortunately, I was hindered for a while by the fact that she was pledging a sorority and therefore otherwise engaged. She was also working and going to school, so there weren't many empty slots in her schedule. But I was well aware that pledge season didn't last forever — and I was nothing if not determined — so I decided to bide my time . . . although to be absolutely truthful, I did make it a point on more than one occasion to "accidently" show up in places where I expected her to be and to give her a wave and then offer her the most dazzling smile of which I was physically capable.

And then my time arrived a few very long weeks later when pledge season came to its inevitable end. In the midst of the sorority's celebration over the induction of its newest sisters, I drew together all my courage. Acting as nonchalant as I could (considering that rejection would utterly obliterate my reason to live), I approached the young woman who seemed to hold my future in her slender and very beautiful hands. I gave her the benefit of my now well-rehearsed smile, and then after a little small talk I croaked out an invitation to dinner, one that I had planned to sound casual, almost offhand — sort of debonair. I fear, however, that it really sounded more like someone pleading for the last lifejacket on the *Titanic*.

And then something wonderful happened: she agreed, without even taking any time to think about it. In fact, she didn't just agree, she actually jumped up and down in what I maintain to this very day was joy — a joy that was at least matched and probably exceeded by my own. I didn't realize it then, but came to understand much later, that I was receiving a gift from God that day, a gift that continues to gladden my life even now, one that I hope will be mine for many, many years to come: a soul mate, a person — just the right person — with whom to journey through life.

We went to a Dutch restaurant for our first date (yes, such establishments exist). I don't remember anything about the food other than that we ate something, but we had what I can only describe as a wonderful time. We talked and talked, and we laughed a lot too. I learned a lot about her, and one of the things I learned right off the bat was that every word that came out of her mouth was fascinating. I learned about her nursing studies. I learned she was at Steubenville primarily because her mother worked at the university, and that meant an all-important tuition waiver for Kathi. I learned that she was a Wesleyan. I learned we had other things in common; one such thing was that she, too, was from Toronto. Her Toronto, however, was a small town in Ohio, just north of Steubenville, rather than in Ontario. What greater sign could the heavens give me that we were meant for each other than that we came from different places with the same name?

So we started dating, Kathi and I, started becoming part of each other's lives in little ways at first and then in slightly bigger ones. Soon, without my even noticing exactly when it happened, I realized it was becoming difficult for me to imagine my life without her. Then — much to my amazement and joy — I began not even wanting to imagine my life without her. I was hooked, and I loved being hooked. I began to hope never to become unhooked.

COMING INTO FOCUS

And I was becoming hooked in a different way as well, a less obvious but no less important way. My second attempt at Steubenville was having a profound effect on me in more ways than one. Perhaps I had marinated in the Catholicism of the place long enough for some of it to have seeped into my psyche. Perhaps the added few years of maturity were having their effect. I can't say for sure. All I can say is that I was no longer the aggressive and slightly confrontational non-Catholic that I had been the first time around.

I didn't feel that the Catholic culture that surrounded me was quite as alien as I had before. Catholic things were somehow more tolerable, if no less strange. I had even given up ducking the holy water that was occasionally flung here and there throughout the dorms and other buildings. I just walked through the deluge like someone walking through a spring rain. When a few drops of it touched me, I discovered it didn't cause my Protestant body to burst into flames or even to writhe in torment; in fact, it felt … okay. Sometimes it actually felt good, and I caught myself wondering a couple of times if there could really be something holy about it after all.

During this period, I found that I was sort of dropping my guard. It was as if for the first time I grasped the fact that I didn't have to be defensive all the time, didn't have to be the single-handed defender of the Reformation in a hotbed of popery — which was a real load off my shoulders, since my knowledge of the Reformation was pretty shaky anyway.

And by the way, I eventually did open the door of the campus chapel and take a look inside. It was not extraordinarily beautiful, but nice somehow, and peaceful. I stood there at the threshold and just stared inside for a few minutes, sniffing the air in a futile attempt to detect the scent of incense, even though I wasn't entirely sure what Catholic incense actually smelled like since we Presbyterians didn't use any kind of incense at all. I still didn't go all the way in: I wasn't ready. But something in me had changed, for I was at least ready to stand at the threshold, at the boundary line. And, amazingly, it didn't seem like such a terrible place to be.

Kathi, I must make very clear, was a big part of this imperceptible and rather glacier-like transformation on my part. She was, in fact, a major element among a whole series of events and people who were leading me on a path that I still didn't realize I was walking. When I met her, she was taking a course in the foundations of Scripture, and she had a professor, who, although Catholic, was very good about explaining both the Catholic and Protestant understandings of things. He showed real respect for his Protestant students, and he made it clear that you didn't always have to take an either/or approach to these questions, that sometimes both/and was the best way to view things. He showed that sometimes the Catholic and Protestant approaches to theological questions did not stand on opposite ends of a spectrum glaring at each other angrily, that sometimes they actually could be reconciled — that sometimes they weren't all that different to begin with.

She spoke to me of this from time to time. At first, it made me mildly uncomfortable, and I came close to wondering if she was actually "Protestant enough," although those silly thoughts soon took flight and never returned. Just looking into her bright blue eyes (which had become one of my favorite pastimes) was enough to tell me that this young woman was "everything enough" for me.

I discovered that Kathi's attitude toward Catholicism was softer and kinder than mine, which shouldn't have been a great surprise, as she was and remains a softer and kinder person. When I would lapse into an occasional aren't-these-Catholics-just-too-weird-for-words tirade, she would quickly silence me, never harshly but always firmly. How could I criticize what this angel of perfection would not? How could I let her imagine that I was harsh or dismissive in my opinions of others? Without ever knowing it, Kathi was making me take a look — a rather hard look — at my own biases, my own rushes to judgment. I didn't always like what I saw.

Kathi, by the way, was not the only one required to take courses in theology. I had no choice but to participate as well. One of mine dealt with Christian moral principles, a topic that I'm sure my father would have approved of wholeheartedly for me. I entered it with my usual reluctance when it came to things Catholic, but the reluctance began to diminish rather quickly.

As I said, something inside me was changing, and for the first time I was beginning to look beneath the surface of things. I don't want to say I was in search of the deep things of life — at least not consciously — but I seemed to be in search of something more than fun and games, and something more than just financial success and security. Some vague stirrings within me were making me a little uncomfortable with my status quo from time to time. Almost against my will I began to find the readings for my theology course interesting, intriguing, and one or two actually seemed, well ... almost exciting.

I did well in that course (I say that with a little pride, even today), and I really felt that I learned something, that it gave me things to think about, to ponder. It also made me begin to see Catholicism in a different light. I realized for the first time — and only slightly against my will — that the Catholic Church is not the slapdash enterprise I had assumed it to be, that it wasn't just a bunch of loosely connected ideas or poorly reasoned and unbiblical doctrines buttressed with a bunch of archaic superstitions. On the contrary, it seemed to hold together, to form a structure that was strong and stable, one that actually made sense. Who would have thought it?

ETHICAL THINKING

And if you think that first theology course had me tottering on the boundary line — half in danger of accidently falling into the chapel (so to speak) — let me tell you that the next one nearly knocked me off my feet.

It was to be a course in ethics, and it had two things going for it, at least from my point of view. The first was that ethics seemed a fairly neutral thing for a Protestant to study in a Catholic college. The second was that Kathi was also scheduled to take the course, and I had reached the point where anyplace that Kathi happened to be was a place that I wanted to be as well.

So I looked forward to my new course in ethics, figuring we'd be discussing life-or-death situations, just-war theory, the pros and cons of capital punishment, business ethics in the contemporary world — all sorts of good stuff that would give me ample opportunity to impress Kathi with my brilliant and incisive classroom discussion.

The problem was that when I actually got to the class, I discovered that the course was to have a narrower focus than I expected — and a very Catholic one at that (surprise!). We were to embark on a very detailed and painstaking semester-long study of some papal document that had a name I kept forgetting because it was in Latin, a language I had never studied.

"*Humanae Vitae*," Kathi kept reminding me.

"*Humanae Vitae*," I repeated dully, wondering what it could be about and if it would give me the opportunity to shine, as I was hoping to.

"It's about birth control," Kathi said.

"It's about what?" I demanded, hoping my ears were playing tricks on me.

"You heard me: birth control, contraception. The moral dimensions of those things."

"Moral dimensions? What moral dimensions? I'm out of here. We've got to find a different course, and fast."

Well, I would have dropped the course if I could have, and I would have pulled Kathi out of that class with me, even if I had to do it by brute force. "What a nonsensical topic," I told her, myself, and anyone who would listen on campus or off. "Why do I have to spend part of my time in college studying what is a complete non-issue — at least to anyone who doesn't live in the dark ages?

"These Catholics ..." I continued, but my words drifted off to nothingness as I noted the stern look Kathi was sending my way.

So we spent a semester reading and analyzing what Pope Paul VI had written about human life and its transmission, on the sacredness of the marital act, on the moral problems with taking steps to thwart that act from achieving its natural goal. In the beginning, I complained bitterly, of course, especially when Kathi was not within earshot. Being from a Protestant background and having uncritically imbibed the ideas and opinions of the contemporary culture, I thought of contraception as an unmitigated good for everyone. But step by slow step something was happening to me as I took that course, and I believe it was the thing that God wanted to happen to me. I believe it was the reason that I had somehow ended up in a place like Steubenville not once, but twice.

"What happened?" you may ask. It was simply this: The reasoning in *Humanae Vitae* began to make sense to me, and I don't just mean that I was willing to grant the pope this or that point, although that's the way it started. I mean that the more I studied, the more convinced I became that *Humanae Vitae* made perfect sense — was right in its entirety. I couldn't find any loopholes in it — and God knows I tried — but strangely and even inexplicably I began to find something else in it, something attractive, something almost beautiful … something (dare I say it?) almost, well, holy.

Although I certainly didn't know it at the time, I would say now that I was receiving some special grace, a grace that was being mediated to me through that course, through the words on the page that I was reading and the lectures I was hearing. It was a grace that was causing my worldview to change in certain ways. It was allowing old ideas and prejudices to begin to crumble so that new possibilities of thought could become open to me — so that a whole new world could open up to me, one that had been there all the time but which I had not noticed or perhaps simply had not *cared enough* to notice.

I did notice one thing, however: that in the midst of that semester-long course I had somehow strayed from my carefully maintained boundary line; slipping accidently off the threshold, I had stumbled a foot or two into the chapel itself. It was a strange but not altogether unwelcome feeling. In reading *Humanae Vitae*, I had discovered something important and exciting in that most unlikely of places, the Catholic Church. The more I thought about it, the more it seemed doubtful that this document was a total fluke.

In other words, I came to the conclusion that it was unlikely that *Humanae Vitae* could be brilliant and incisive and the rest of the Catholic Church could be total nonsense. So, since I had slipped into the chapel anyway, I decided

I might as well explore it a little — you know, just to see what other interesting items these Catholics might have lying around.

LATE TO CHURCH

Well, I suppose that after reading that last section, you expected my next stop to be the baptismal font or at least the book-lined study of some understanding priest, where I would haltingly discuss the possibility of conversion. Nope. Rome wasn't built in a day, and apparently getting to Rome was not something I was capable of accomplishing in a day — or, for that matter, a year or even a couple of years.

I guess I was easily distractible, which made a certain amount of sense, considering that I was being pulled in three directions at once. Maybe a better way of saying it is that I had three competing foci in my life: my studies, at which I was absolutely determined to succeed; my relationship with Kathi, without which I had no reason to succeed; and my religious questioning, which was becoming steadily more important. Yet it was something that I had a real talent for putting on the back burner, at just the right temperature, to keep it nice and warm without ever boiling over. My experiences studying theology from a Catholic perspective were provocative and sometimes even tantalizing.

I can't deny that almost against my will I felt a pull in the direction of the Catholic Church, but you have to recall that my dad was a Presbyterian minister and I looked up to him tremendously. If the Catholic Church was right, if it had as much to offer as it sometimes seemed to, then why did my dad stay so firmly entrenched in Protestantism? What did he know that I didn't? Why should I consider making a change when he, who knew so much more about these matters, did not? (I marvel at the preceding few sentences, for they show how little I understood my parents, and especially my father, when I was young. If I had really spent the time to learn what was going on in his mind and the depths of his soul during that period, I might have done things differently — but more on that later.)

So I didn't actually retreat to the boundary line again, but neither did I fully enter the chapel, at least not for several years, except to wander through it as an interested but occasional tourist of the sort you sometimes see in great cathedrals, their baseball caps on their heads and their guidebooks in their hands. When my senior year rolled around, however, the pace of things leading me to the Church began to pick up somewhat.

The first thing that happened was that my parents did something utterly bizarre: they actually moved to Steubenville for a year. No! I know what you're thinking, but you're wrong. It wasn't to keep an eye on me. It was for my father to take a position as visiting professor in the business department. Of course, I felt exactly what any college student would feel under the circumstance, but I managed to get over it pretty quickly, especially since they had made the move for my benefit: the resulting reduced tuition made it possible to cover all my bills without having to mortgage the house and my having to become an indentured servant for the first ten years after graduation.

So I'm not going to tell you that having my parents living in Steubenville and my father teaching at my college was an all-fun-and-games sort of thing, because it wasn't. But in certain ways it did bring us together. It also made me increasingly aware of my father's very respectful and even admiring regard for both Catholicism in general and individual Catholics in particular. He seemed interested in their opinions, at times almost fascinated by their ideas. And in observing this I began to feel as if he was tacitly giving me his approval to further investigate the Catholic Church, this strange institution that was by turns off-putting and attractive — sometimes very off-putting and often extremely attractive.

We sometimes had conversations, my father and I, in which we compared the Protestant approach to that of the Catholic Church. We discussed the many conflicting ideas that permeated Protestantism in all its different strains and divisions, the fact that each moral problem had to be addressed over and over as a result of the Protestant lack of a central authority. We talked about the fact that even supposedly settled theological doctrines could sometimes be set aside by a mere majority vote.

And these conversations began to make sense to me, to make the Catholic position look good, solid — levelheaded. They made me recall my reading of *Humanae Vitae* and how elegantly simple and unavoidable the logic of it was. I began to yearn for that clarity, for the assurance that "yes" always meant "yes" and "no" always meant "no." But just when I began to believe that the Catholic Church might be the place for me, all my earlier doubts would come rushing back, and I would wonder what freedom there could be in such a Church, what the role of conscience actually was, and if one could truly remain an individual or had to be a total conformist.

And these conversations, as well as many internal debates went on for some time, probably long enough to try God's patience, except that God has infinite patience — which was a good thing for me. I believe they were in some way a necessary step along the path that God had put me on, a stage that simply had to last as long as it had to last. Perhaps it was just a time for me to mull over the questions, if not to arrive at any answers; a time to discard the last remnants of my adolescent approach to life, to people, to faith.

And I really was doing some growing during this period. The primary catalyst for this was my relationship with Kathi. Because of that, I was thinking of the future, not just in terms of financial success but in terms of real commitment. Like many men, I was sort of dragged kicking and screaming out of adolescence by finding the right person, by thinking seriously about the possibility of marriage and family.

So I never mentioned the "C" word during this period, never spoke about conversion except in the abstract, not even with my father, until after I graduated. By this time, and by God's grace, Kathi and I had been married in her small hometown Wesleyan church, making me the happiest and luckiest Steubenville graduate of the year. (Who needs Phi Beta Kappa when you can have that?) The wedding marked a culmination of my enthusiastic pursuit of this young woman whose beauty had utterly captivated me, and it marked the beginning of our lives together — in other words, I could start breathing easy: we were committed to each other and that meant I could stop worrying about losing her. At the end of the academic year, my parents returned to Toronto, and Kathi and I began our lives as newly minted adults.

Chapter 7

Spiritual Nomads

"The Israelites are wandering about aimlessly in the land. The wilderness has closed in on them."

— Exodus 14:3

After graduation we moved to Cleveland, Ohio, which was strategically situated between the two Torontos, Kathi's and mine, and we began the life that we thought we should be living. I started (or re-started) my career, this time with a great CPA firm, and far more important, our family began growing rapidly. Within two years and eight months, we were the parents of three children — no twins, just raw chemistry, youthful enthusiasm, and a deeply influential reading of *Humanae Vitae*. We were living a good life, a happy life, and a life that was very rewarding. The difference that children can make in the way you view the world is impossible to comprehend until you experience it, and I was experiencing it and loving every second of it.

I was caught up in my growing family and my work, absorbed in the people I loved and the things I loved doing, yet once again my religious questions resurfaced in a vaguely reproachful way. My attraction to Catholicism remained, but once I was out of Franciscan University it had become easier to ignore because I was no longer confronted by the Church at every turn. We began searching for a church home, of course, but nothing really satisfied, and we became spiritual nomads. First, we went to a Full Gospel church with some friends. That place was charismatic in a big way, which was not totally unfamiliar to us, as Franciscan University had certainly more than a touch of the charismatic about it. We both liked the people. They were warm, friendly, and full of enthusiasm, but our time at Steubenville had done its work and we found that we wanted — needed — more than that.

Doctrinally, that church was hard to pin down and that bothered us. It bothered us so much, in fact, that we bid the place a fond farewell and continued our wanderings, eventually trying a Baptist, a Methodist, and then a Presbyterian church. None seemed the answer to our prayers, so we fretted for a while and then decided to do something daring, something outrageous, something both of us had wanted to do but neither had felt comfortable mentioning. Hold on to your hats, because here it comes: We decided to go to a Catholic church. So one Sunday we did, and you know what? We didn't even wear disguises.

Once again I've led you to the point when my conversion should be just around the corner, and once again I must disappoint, for the Catholic church we attended was the one in which I was eventually baptized and, if you've been reading attentively, you'll know that my first experience there was not compelling. The music was dreary, the homily was uninspiring, the people seemed cold, and the priest appeared to be just going through the motions. I have to say I was not impressed, which was a deep disappointment, because I *wanted* to be impressed; I wanted to be moved. In short, I wanted to feel that sense of the holy that I had felt a few times at Steubenville.

If truth be told, I wanted to find a way to make that mysterious something part of my life. I also wanted to see something of that startling clarity, that depth of perception, which I had encountered while studying *Humanae Vitae*. But I didn't — not even close. I was like someone who was expecting a banquet and was served an overcooked cheeseburger and soggy fries instead. What I did see, however, was something very familiar to me from Sunday mornings in Steubenville: the congregation bolting for the door before the last hymn was sung.

So, not too many weeks later, Kathi and I joined a Christian and Missionary Alliance church. Theologically, it was an offshoot of the Presbyterian Church, which made me feel right at home. It also, as the name implies, has a real missionary spirit. My parents had been missionaries in Nigeria, so this, too, made me feel that we had found a good church home — even if it wasn't the right home, which was a doubt that kept nibbling at me like a persistent mosquito, one I kept trying to swat but never could quite manage to squash.

We enjoyed that church and the people who attended it. It was a good place and comfortable in many ways, pleasing both Kathi and me. For a while — a rather long while, actually — I kept telling myself that such a church would be enough for me, that I had no reason to look any further. I worked hard at convincing myself that my peculiar attraction to Catholicism had been a temporary aberration and was now over, a phase that had come and gone. Graduating from Steubenville and entering the real world meant leaving it behind. For a long time I think I actually believed this … sort of.

ROLE REVERSALS

The problem was that my dad — the one who always seemed to have a knack for shaking up my life — was hard at work at doing so again. After completing his year on the faculty at Franciscan, he returned to Toronto where, among other things, he owned a computer business that sold a product he had created called the "Findit Bible." It was a CD containing several different translations of the Bible that could be searched instantly. Although we take this type of thing for granted now, at the time this was cutting-edge technology. These electronic Bibles began to sell pretty well over in Europe. Amazingly, this resulted in an invitation from — of all places — the Vatican. So while Kathi and I were still seeking answers, my dad jetted to Rome for a weeklong trip that produced an audience with Pope John Paul II and a lasting friendship with Archbishop (later Cardinal) John Foley.

It also produced an article that my father wrote on the subject of Christian unity, which was published by the *Presbyterian Record*, the denominational magazine of The Presbyterian Church in Canada. In turn, this article resulted in a huge amount of flak for my dad, as some hardline Protestants called him to task for being — shall we say — just a bit too friendly toward Rome. He was a Clerk of the General Assembly of The Presbyterian Church in Canada, so his picture on the front cover of the magazine, shaking hands with Pope John Paul II, probably didn't help. Some of the responses to the article bordered on hate mail: "Doesn't Dr. Lowry know that the pope is the Antichrist?"

In the midst of my own struggles, my dad's approach to things converged with mine. At around the same time that his article was generating waves among Presbyterians, I found that I was generating a few waves myself in my Bible study group at my church. My waves came about seemingly accidently, but to this very day I maintain that they are proof positive that God has a sense of humor — a slightly offbeat one, I'll grant you, but it's definitely there. What other explanation could there be for the onetime-Protestant bad boy of Steubenville to suddenly find himself cast in the role of sole defender of the Catholic faith in a roomful of his fellow Protestants?

I've never been a shrinking violet, and so when some condescending, incorrect, or even ignorant statements about the Catholic Church were uttered (which they were with more frequency than you might suspect), I felt it incumbent upon me — the one in the room with a degree from a Catholic college after all — to share the knowledge I had gained and make a gentle but firm correction. I was pleased with myself and thought this worked well, although it seemed to generate a number of bemused looks aimed in my direction.

As time went on, however, some statements that I took to be genuinely anti-Catholic were made. Predictably, these caused my corrections to become a little less gentle and a little more firm, which, in turn, caused the bemused looks to become a little more frequent and a little more intense, until after a while I was beginning to feel kind of like Paul Scofield playing St. Thomas More in one of the later scenes in *A Man for All Seasons* — you know, the ones where you can hear the wood for the scaffold being nailed together in the background.

Except that I wasn't Paul Scofield or any other actor, because I wasn't playing a role. I meant it when I found myself arguing against the very same ideas that I had held for most of my life — the very same ideas that had once fueled my feelings of superiority at Steubenville. That realization confused me. It was disorienting to discover myself fighting for something that I had attacked more than a few times in the past.

What was even more disorienting was the discovery that my attraction to Catholicism had not waned one bit since I had left college but had somehow grown stronger without my noticing it. Even my regard for Franciscan University itself had increased. The party-school illusion had gradually been replaced with a deep sense of respect and admiration for what turned out to be a dynamic school of sanctification. As a result, I found I was not merely correcting factual errors in that Bible study group but arguing for something that had become important to me in an oddly personal way. Hearing the Church misrepresented or unfairly criticized actually hurt me. I didn't really grasp why, but something I did grasp — suddenly and fully — was the passion I glimpsed from time to time at Steubenville: the reason why that slightly built, pro-life girl walloped me so hard in the college cafeteria and the reason why so many people dragged themselves out of bed early on dismal Sunday mornings to enter a weird-looking chapel.

It wasn't abstract. It was personal, and it could hurt! It was something that took hold of you, of something deep inside you — and, whether I liked it or not, it seemed to be taking hold of something inside *me*!

DARKNESS BEFORE DAWN

That realization hit me like a ton of bricks, and it made me unsure of everything, of who I really was. Things that had seemed stable were now somehow in motion — in turmoil. A turbulence was beginning to swirl around me and in me. I tried to suppress it, and sometimes I thought I had done so, but it refused to be suppressed; it just came back over and over again until it eventually knocked me off the boundary line on which I was so carefully perched and swept me all the way into the chapel — into my home.

But I wasn't just getting swept along; I was getting into more and more hot water with my Protestant friends. The Protestant ideas that had seemed so natural and sturdy to me now seemed increasingly shaky and undependable. What had once seemed incontrovertible truth now seemed shot through with flaws and unanswered (and even unasked) questions. I began to discuss religion more and more with people, and I think I did so in search of some solid ground on which to reestablish the foundation of my Protestant faith, but the ground kept crumbling beneath me.

I continued to discover flaws in the thinking of my Protestant friends. A more subtle person might have kept those flaws to himself, but I was desperate and not naturally given to subtlety anyway, so I kept pointing them out, hoping for satisfying answers. I rarely got them. What I got were more bemused looks, especially when I started articulating the Catholic position on this or that issue and saying things like, "That makes a lot of sense, don't you think?"

This sort of thing reached its culmination during lunch with a friend one day. He generously offered to "disciple" me but spent the entire lunch quoting Bible verses at me in a very vigorous effort to support his "once saved always saved" convictions (yet another topic about which there were a plethora of opinions among my sincere Christian friends). I knew that there was a not-very-distant time in my life when this sort of conversation would not have bothered me much. But that time was past, and his arguments seemed to be a lot of pointless tail chasing, nothing more than another attempt to build a foundation on shifting sand, on personal opinion, on the stitching together of Scripture verses never meant to go together.

So I explained that to him, and I also explained — perhaps in more detail than was strictly necessary — the

Catholic position on salvation. I couldn't match him in quoting biblical verses from memory, but I found it a little too enjoyable poking holes in his shaky doctrine. The lunch didn't end as well as it could have if I had kept my mouth shut, and needless to say, we didn't go through with the discipleship process.

During this period I was beginning to see many things differently. It was almost as if a new worldview had been incubating in me somewhere and was now ready to spring to life. The diversity of opinion, the multiplicity of views that had once seemed the glory of Protestantism, began to seem more like a fatal flaw to me, a cacophony rather than the vast creative dialogue that I always supposed it to be.

"Our souls are restless until they rest in Thee," wrote St. Augustine, and that, I realized, is what I wanted to do: to rest in something stable. At twenty-five, I'd had my fill of being restless, of being buffeted by the endless contradictions and competing opinions of Protestantism. I wanted to rest in something that could reflect or at least hint at the infinite stability of God.

There aren't too many places you can go if that's what you want. In fact, at last count there's only one.

THE ROSARY — WARINESS TO WONDER

So what does a Protestant who thinks he's really a closet Catholic do when he feels compelled to out himself? Why, he goes straight to a former Protestant who's now a bona fide Catholic, of course. My dad and I had listened to a tape of Scott Hahn, and that tape deeply impressed me. After hearing it, I called Scott and actually struck up a kind of friendship, proving that it sometimes pays to be bold.

Scott actually volunteered to become my sponsor if I wanted to join the Church — a shocking idea at the time that he announced it. But I was ready now, or at least I thought I was. The first time we met in person, he pulled a rosary out of his pocket and put it in my hand. It was the first rosary I ever held, much less owned, and I was a little wary of it in the beginning. Sometimes I'd just hold it or let the beads slip between my fingers; sometimes I'd just stare at the crucifix that hung from it. Gradually, however, I began to investigate what you were supposed to do with this strange device. And then one day (when nobody was looking), I took a deep breath and actually did it.

Okay, so I'd like to write here that I had a mystical experience that would have given St. Bernadette Soubirous, to whom Mary appeared at Lourdes, a run for her money … but I didn't. However, it wasn't bad at all. No lightning struck me, but the repetition of the same words, the same prayers, seemed to create a nice flow, one that could carry you along if you let it. When I was done, I decided that I would pray the Rosary again someday. And I did. And then I did it again, and again, and again, and then something strange happened: I began to look forward to my private time with the Rosary, with Jesus. And not only with Jesus, of course, but with His mother, whom I had ignored for a very long time. I discovered it was quite nice, really, to finally make Mary's acquaintance. It also marked a turning point, because within weeks of beginning to pray the Rosary, I discovered that I wanted nothing more than to become a Catholic. In fact, I couldn't bear not being a Catholic. I was somehow smack dab in the middle of the chapel, and I wasn't even looking for the exit sign.

So the Rosary became a very powerful part of my prayer life, one that I wasn't shy about mentioning to my friends; but since many of my friends were part of my Bible study group, the inevitable happened. I was read the riot act and told that I was leading my family down the wrong path — that's the path that leads straight to hell, in case you haven't figured it out. After that, I was basically shunned, excommunicated — which was no fun at all. Later I learned that Kathi was actually being counseled to divorce me because of my determination to become Catholic.

All of that was a lot to deal with. At any other point in my life, I would have given up in the face of it. The thought of losing Kathi was like a fate worse than death for me. By that time we'd been together for a while, and I felt like we were cemented. Losing her would be like having a part of me violently ripped away — the good part, the part that includes my heart! So I tried to give up my desire to become a Catholic. I tried really hard. The problem was that I couldn't do it. In fact, I couldn't give up anything: not the Catholic Church, not my rosary, and certainly not Kathi. In the deepest part of my soul, I knew in some vague way that she'd never leave me — or at least I thought I knew it. Just to make sure, I turned to Jesus and His mother in the Rosary again, which was the only thing I could do because it was the Rosary that had gotten me into this predicament. The Rosary had pushed me over the edge. Now I was counting on the Rosary to catch me as I fell.

And somehow it did. I don't know how, but it did. Kathi and I talked and talked. Some of those talks were not easy, but they were valuable. She was still very unsure about the Catholic Church. She was on the path into it to be sure, but she was a few steps behind me (I've always been a fast walker). Kathi wasn't ready to make a move and didn't want to do so, at least not yet. Frankly, she was tired of having our lives upset in the way they were being upset. She wanted some kind of normalcy, and I couldn't blame her.

But despite her hesitancy, she expressed a very deep and beautiful love. Kathi agreed to attempt what I was ready for and she was not. Out of love she decided to accompany me on the path that it seemed I was destined to walk. So, hand in hand, we turned our backs on everything we had known, and together we walked into the unknown — and that means into a Catholic church, the one in which we were eventually baptized. We spoke to a couple of priests, who turned out to be kind and understanding. We signed up for an RCIA course that ran from September until Easter. We studied; we learned. I asked too many questions; she asked too few (but together it sort of evened out). We went to Mass — and eventually we started praying together, just simple prayers at first, but Catholic ones, with wording that seemed strange to us.

None of this was easy. I began to become aware of a tension growing between us, a tension that hadn't been there before and had come into existence solely because I was doing what I felt I had to do and I was pulling Kathi along with me. I didn't know how to deal with this except through prayer; so that's what I did, returning to the Rosary and laying my problems at the feet of Christ and His mother.

As the weeks passed, the praying continued, and then Kathi gave me a remarkable gift. It was another rosary, this one for her. Tentatively, and probably not wholeheartedly, she began to pray it with me. She learned the various mysteries; she picked up the right rhythm. Perhaps in the beginning she was just mouthing the prayers in order to please me, but beginnings don't last forever, and the Rosary has a way of asserting itself whether you want it to or not. One night I saw Kathi, the rosary in her hands, the beads slipping gracefully between her beautiful fingers, and I knew she wasn't doing anything to please me. She was giving herself over to this most beautiful and most Catholic of prayers. I could feel it, and when I felt it I breathed easily for the first time in a long, long time.

As we prayed the Rosary together that night, I knew we were no longer at the boundary line. I was no longer gazing into the chapel from afar. We were coming home, and we were coming home together — arriving at the place God wanted us to be. I looked at Kathi that night and felt I would burst with love. It was, however, hard to see her because my eyes were somehow too wet. So as I gazed at her she shimmered, and we sat there together, beads in our hands, in the presence of our Lord Jesus Christ and His Blessed Mother.

And although I didn't quite realize it that night, we were at home for the first time ever.

~

So, that's it. It's how God drew me into the Church. I'm sure a lot of people have similar tales, and I'm equally sure that enormous numbers of people have stories that are radically different. We're all unique, after all, and because of that God deals with us in ways suited to our uniqueness. Each of us is offered a path to our heavenly Father — and, kind of like snowflakes, no two of those paths are identical, although many resemble each other in certain ways.

Over time, I have had occasion to know others on the path of conversion. In fact, through the Coming Home Network, I've encountered many such people and spoken to them in depth about their particular paths to God. Through these conversations and my own experiences, I gradually became aware of certain problems that often confront converts no matter what their individual path and no matter whether they come to the Church from a different faith tradition or the secular world.

Actually, I probably shouldn't call them "problems," for that's not really what they are. They're more like hurdles that many or even most people have to clear on their way into the Church. They can also be called "stumbling blocks" along the path. They're the things that require the most adjustment, the things that remind a convert that he sometimes has to adopt a new way of thinking, a new way of seeing things.

I think there are at least seven (or eight) big ones — hurdles or stumbling blocks — that most people must confront. The majority are very specific to the Church, like Mary and the saints. This type of stumbling block involves the acceptance of new and sometimes strange-seeming doctrines and dogmas. They're a challenge to a Protestant, but they can be overcome. When the deepest part of the soul finally assents to them, you have arrived at a very beautiful place. A couple of the hurdles, however, are more general, like the need to accept authority and deal with imperfections within the Church. These stumbling blocks confront not just Catholics or people entering the Church; they confront everyone. Yet I think they resonate in a special way for Catholics. They are a deep part of the Catholic soul, and so anyone who hopes for real conversion must address them in a special way.

I had to deal with each one of these stumbling blocks, and I probably continue to deal with them. Some were kind of difficult. Others were confusing. However, overcoming them, one after another, produced a wonderful feeling, for each time I did it was as if I was entering more deeply into Catholic life and becoming closer to God.

So here's a look at those stumbling blocks, a look that is sometimes lighthearted because I have a sense of humor and I suspect you do too — and God has the best sense of humor of all.

PART II

TURNING STUMBLING BLOCKS INTO STEPPING-STONES

or

How All Those Weird Things
About Catholicism Turn Out to Make Sense
and Actually Bring You Closer to God

Chapter 8

First Stumbling Block: The Eucharist

Jesus said to them, "Amen, amen, I say to you, unless you eat the flesh of the Son of Man and drink his blood, you do not have life within you."

— John 6:53

During the months leading up to my baptism, conversion was sometimes described to me as a journey that isn't finished until our earthly lives are finished — it's ongoing. I liked that image because it made sense to me. It also made me feel like I was on board a ship on my way to someplace important. I could almost feel my hand on the rudder as I stood beneath billowing white sails, heading into uncharted territories filled with promise.

I still like the image. Only now I know it's the wrong one. In the beginning, I guess I didn't quite understand that although I may have been on the journey of a lifetime, my hand wasn't on the rudder at all. I guess I was just a little too human, which means a little too reluctant, to cede control to anyone — even to God. I had to learn to accept the fact that my job had to do with learning a new way of seeing things, of letting a new understanding of life, of the world, of just about everything, slowly seep into me until it took root, burrowing deep into my soul and changing me in ways

I could never quite anticipate. In other words, my job was not to chart a course but rather to remove the blocks, to let resistance fall away, to open myself to something that was in some ways quite familiar yet in others very, very new. In short, it was my job to surrender the navigation to surer hands.

Now, all that surrendering can be difficult for anyone who has been raised in our modern (or is it postmodern?) world. After all, we are taught that we are autonomous beings, possessing majestic and indomitable wills. We are also taught that it is our nature to control our future and the world around us — which means we're supposed to control pretty much everything, I guess. We are the center and determiner of our lives, the maker of our very selves. All that sounds pretty grand, or at least grandiose, but there's a sad "fact" that goes along with it: This world we create is often superficial, lacking both depth and meaning, at least any meaning other than the one we choose to impose upon it at a given moment. In other words, the current "truth" has it that what we cannot see or touch, measure or calculate, doesn't exist, and what science can't capture and shove under a microscope just isn't there at all.

Every convert to Catholicism has these ideas swimming around in his or her mind subtly, or not so subtly, influencing the way religious truth is perceived and understood, and I was no exception. I definitely don't want to criticize unjustly the Protestant world that formed me, but I have to say that many Christian denominations have accepted this way of thinking too completely, resulting in a flattening of the great Christian mysteries, a demotion of fact to symbol, of ineffable reality to cool and distant abstraction that the human mind can wrap itself around.

That's one of the big reasons the Catholic Church seemed so foreign, so weird, and so incomprehensible to me when I first encountered it at Steubenville. On some level, I grasped that the Catholic Church was drastically out of step with the world as I knew it. Later, as I grew closer and closer to the Church, I began to realize that it was not just out of step: it *completely rejected* the dominant worldview — and if that doesn't give a potential convert pause, not much will.

Gradually, and with some difficulty, I came to see that the Catholic Church is deeply wedded to the idea that what we can see, touch, measure, and calculate is but the tip of the iceberg, that our minds are much feebler than we want to believe, and that reality is far deeper than we want to admit. I think you can sort of sum it up by saying that the proper Catholic response to the scientist who has just discovered a new galaxy or some astonishing secret of DNA might be: "Wow. That's really amazing, but you ain't seen nothin' yet."

Which finally brings me to the topic at hand: the greatest and most ineffable mystery of all, the one many of my Protestant friends are least likely to be able to wrap their heads around, the one that most clearly and loudly proclaims, "You ain't seen nothin' yet." Hold on to your hats, because here it comes: the Holy Eucharist.

YOU ARE WHO YOU EAT

In the Holy Eucharist, the Catholic Church makes an absolutely incredible claim — one that our contemporary world would consider sheer lunacy if it ever bothered to think about it at all. The claim is no less than this: During the Mass (each and every Mass), reality is altered; the barriers between heaven and earth crumble; God in Christ offers Himself to us and enters our innermost being so intimately that He becomes closer to us than we are to ourselves. He actually feeds us with His very being — the Divine Being!

Now, if you've been Catholic all your life, maybe that doesn't sound strange to you. But if it doesn't sound strange to you, then maybe you haven't given it much real thought. Coming from a Protestant background, I felt like I might never recover when the time came to consider this one. Let me explain.

In my father's Presbyterian church, we had quarterly (later monthly) Communion services, and they were very dignified affairs. Ushers moved solemnly through the congregation, holding round trays with holes in them. Each hole contained a tiny glass; half the glasses were filled with wine and the other half with grape juice. They also passed around separate trays of cut-up white bread, each about the size of a Lego piece. Communion was always taken seriously. I knew it was meaningful, but I never quite got what the real meaning was. I always felt that it was vaguely disappointing, sort of an anticlimax; it was as if something was missing, but I could never figure out what that something was. The whole thing was done with prayerful reverence, but no one believed that Christ was actually present in the bread and wine in a special way. It never occurred to me to believe something like that either, or even to consider the possibility.

If I grasped what was meant by Communion at all, I guess I understood it as an act of remembrance, certainly not a celebration of particular presence. This feeling was intensified when, at the end of the service, I saw the leftover bread thrown into the trash and the grape juice and wine saved for the next time in a small refrigerator. Our Communion service was a symbolic act, and a meaningful one for many people, but it was not a divine drama, and it involved no intimate contact with the One who gave His life for us. There was no meeting of heaven and earth; there was just bread that was only bread and wine that was nothing but wine.

The Presbyterian version now seems to me like an echo of the sacrament I have come to know. And, by the way, that Presbyterian version and most Protestant versions of the Holy Eucharist are perfectly acceptable to the contemporary mind — the mind that perceives only the tip of the iceberg. It is unthreatening, easily tolerable. But sort of like plastic fruit in a table centerpiece, it cannot feed us in any way or fulfill the great yearnings of our souls.

I recall no preparation or formation for Communion in the Presbyterian Church. It was just something you started to participate in when you were old enough and no longer were sent off to Sunday school while the adults were engaged in worship. Truth be told, I didn't like it very much because it made a long Sunday morning in church even longer for a restless and overly energetic boy. Heck, my dad's sermons were expected to be forty-five minutes long, or else congregants didn't think they got their money's worth! As a result, Communion had little meaning for me. I saw it as simply another item on the Sunday morning agenda, like singing another hymn or reciting another prayer. It was a chore to do, an obligation to fulfill.

That's why learning what the Catholic Church means by the Eucharist was so disorienting, so thrilling, and yet so terrifying for me. In the Catholic Church, the Eucharist is the doorway to the depths of reality — to what is *most real* — to the world that is concealed from our senses and our rational minds. In the Eucharist, God offers us an entrance to His mysterious Kingdom that infinitely exceeds our imaginations. We meet Him; we "commune" with Him in a very literal yet utterly inconceivable way.

In the Eucharist, we must leave our rational minds behind to enter a reality that outstrips our profoundest thoughts, that has nothing to do with our emotions. It doesn't matter what you *feel*; the only thing that matters is *Who* it is — and it is Christ: body, blood, soul, and divinity. It is the gift of self (I love that term), but not just the gift of any self: It is the gift of Christ's own self to us. It is a gift that does the impossible, allowing the finite to touch the infinite — to consume the infinite and so be transformed. The Eucharist permits us, at least for a moment, to become like Mary herself, for in the Eucharist we, too, are allowed to hold infinity, divinity, eternity, within us.

TRUST, EAT, REPEAT

Here's something else to ponder: Both the convert and the cradle Catholic must come to terms with the Eucharist if they are to be truly Catholic to the core. I don't imagine that you can "think" your way to a real acceptance of the Eucharist, but you can "trust" your way to an acceptance and even an understanding of the Eucharist. That's what I meant when I said it is my job as a convert (our job, really, for we are all converts) to let resistance fall away, to simply accept that when we approach the altar we draw near to a love too great to comprehend. It is our job as we make our journey of conversion to allow that love to do its work on us.

And it is our job to permit ourselves to accept the idea that when the priest prays the Eucharistic Prayer, something that transcends time itself is occurring; Christ's sacrifice on Mount Calvary is not being reproduced in any way, but it is being made mysteriously present. After all, God isn't constrained by time and space, and His sacrifice is both definitive and eternal. This collapsing of time is often misunderstood by people from Protestant (and certainly secular) backgrounds, but when it is finally grasped (and it took me a while to grasp it) it helps things fall into place. When I began to understand this "making present" of an event that I had thought was consigned firmly to the past, I also began to see what the Church has always seen: that it is possible to share in that sacrifice of total love, to become a participant rather than a mere onlooker, to try to offer myself, as He offers Himself, and thus to participate in the event that is the source of our redemption.

This act of sharing, I came to understand, propels our conversion forward, not because of anything we do, but because of what we allow to happen to us. In other words, we just need to be open to allowing Him to work in us, and He does this in such a way that it is really *His* action, not ours. The objective reality of What and Who the Eucharist is becomes the primary means of our ongoing conversion, if we but step out of the way and accept it.

I know that some people will find these words extravagant and others will find them absurd. That doesn't bother me. What does bother me, however, is those people who will have no reaction to them at all. It took me a long time to become truly Catholic regarding the Eucharist, and perhaps I'm still working on it. It was an extended journey but an amazingly rewarding one. I see now that the Eucharist is not just the center of my life but the center of all life; it is the reality of the presence of the God who created us and sustains us at every instant. Understanding the Eucharist became for me a source of hope; receiving it became a source of great joy.

I know that is not the case for everyone, and my own experience is no less uneven than anyone else's. It's easy to take for granted that which seems so ... well, humble and unremarkable. There have been more times than I would like to admit when I have been casual or distracted (sometimes juggling a child or two) as I approached the altar. There have even been times when I have received the Eucharist with less reverence than people in my Presbyterian past took their bread and their wine, and this is a fact that saddens me. How could I have been so unaware of the sacred reality that confronted me at that moment? I can't answer that question except to say that I still have a long way to go in my spiritual journey.

My great comfort, however, is the knowledge that regardless of my state of mind, reception of the sacrament is efficacious. It's not real because of me; it's real because of Christ. So whether or not we struggle with the reality of the Eucharist — as perhaps all contemporary people must struggle in one way or another — it's still an invitation to grow in trust and love for Jesus, by opening our hearts and minds to receive Him in a way that is supremely, divinely, beautiful.

TRUE WEALTH

Sometimes in my Protestant past, God seemed distant, ensconced in heaven, cut off from my daily life, and I don't think that's uncommon. That way of thinking can gradually drain the world of holiness, leaving it to secularity, and producing that flatness of which I have already spoken. In becoming Catholic, I have come to understand that God is far closer than I once thought Him to be, that He is really and truly present in many places and events — even when I can't sense Him. Every tabernacle in every Catholic Church pulsates with the Divine Presence. Every Mass is alive with the reality of God. I also see in a clearer way that Christ is encountered in others. How natural this thought becomes when we think of Christ feeding people with His very self.

I fear that some cradle Catholics don't have a sense of this, don't realize what the Church teaches regarding the Eucharist or how important that teaching is. Polls tell us that many Catholics don't believe in the Real Presence, that some don't even understand what the Real Presence is.

In fact, it may seem strange, but I don't think I even knew the word "Eucharist" until my first semester at Steubenville. At that point, a couple of friends and I were walking on campus late at night, and one of them said he heard that people had tried to break into the chapel.

"Why would they do that?" I asked.

"To steal the Eucharist!" was the response.

"The what?" I asked.

"The Eucharist! The body of Christ!"

I had no idea what he meant that night, and it would be years before I did.

But now I know, and this knowledge changes my life. It makes me see the world differently — aware, on some level, of the incredible depth that is beneath me, the imperceptible yet completely real world that supports us all. The Eucharist is a regular reminder of this and a regular entrance into that world. I open myself to Christ in the Eucharist the best I can, and suddenly I touch the holy; I am in the presence of the sacred.

If you are still struggling to accept the Church's amazing claims about what appears to be mere bread and wine, I urge you to stop struggling, and instead let your resistance fall away and accept that Christ wants to come to you in a way too profound for words. Perhaps you cannot draw near to Him, but you can let Him draw near to you; and when you do this, you will discover a world that you cannot see or touch, measure or calculate, but you will have discovered a world that is more real than any you have ever known.

By the way, the same night I was bending awkwardly over the baptismal font, I was thrilled to enter this world, especially with my wife beside me and my parents looking on, with what? Envy? Perhaps it really was envy, because less than a year later, they entered the Church themselves. My dad told me that he had come to believe that the Eucharist was the key to Christian unity — the topic he felt so strongly about and discussed in his article in the *Presbyterian Record* that caused so much controversy. I was honored to serve as my dad's sponsor — and to watch him and my mom receive the precious gift of the Eucharist for the first time.

Chapter 9

Second Stumbling Block: Confession

And when he had said this, he breathed on them and said to them, "Receive the holy Spirit. Whose sins you forgive are forgiven them, and whose sins you retain are retained."
— John 20:22-23

Okay, so you thought we were done with the autobiographical part of this little book. Well, almost but not quite, because I'm about to tell you a little story from my childhood, but first I have to set the scene.

Picture me at a very young age — maybe ten years old. I'm in my bedroom, the door is shut, and I'm kneeling by my bed, hands clasped in prayer. My eyes are closed because I have the vague idea that closing your eyes so tightly that it almost hurts somehow intensifies your praying ability — puts it in the fast lane, so to speak. I'm as filled with remorse as a ten-year-old can be because I've done something terribly wrong, so wrong that (after a lengthy and quite unpleasant lecture) my parents have banished me to my bedroom and suggested I ask (or better, "beg") God for forgiveness.

Following orders as best I can, I'm overflowing with promises to the Almighty to mend my ways, to be good, to obey my parents, to not break anything (especially anything expensive and difficult to replace), to come home on time rather than half an hour later, to do my homework, to — well, you get the idea.

Now the story: This praying goes on and on for *at least* a few minutes, my promises becoming more and more extravagant as the seconds tick by until, finally, I'm all prayed out. I can't think of any more items to offer God in bargaining for forgiveness. My knees are also beginning to hurt, and although I sincerely hope God hasn't noticed, I'm getting a little bored. And then — holding my breath — I ask God for a sign that everything will be all right between us from this point on.

For another minute or so I stay there, not moving, my eyes still tightly shut. Why? Because I'm giving God time to decide on an appropriate sign and then to actually produce it. Slowly, I open my left eye and scan the room. Everything seems to be exactly as it was before I began to pray. I open my right eye and perform another scan. It offers similarly disappointing results.

As the seconds continue to pass, I get up, go to the window, look out — but find nothing out of the ordinary. A bird flies by, producing a brief moment of excitement. Could that be the sign? I try hard to convince myself that it is, but I finally decide that it's probably too much to ask a robin to be a sign of divine forgiveness. Besides, birds fly by all the time; God wouldn't choose such an everyday occurrence when He could give a really good sign, like a solar eclipse or a snowstorm in the middle of summer. Didn't Moses get a burning bush? Noah got a flood that consumed the earth, but that wasn't supposed to happen again. And Jonah got a free ride inside a whale, right? Something like that would be a perfect sign!

An anguish-filled eternity later (about fifteen minutes), my parents release me from my prison. Relieved, I grin at them, for they have forgiven me, and I am once more a member in good standing of the family. All is finally right with the Lowrys — but what about with God?

And that was a problem I had to deal with not just as a child but throughout my entire Protestant life. Forgiveness was a big issue with me. I was never quite sure that God heard my pleas for pardon, never certain that He had granted them, never clear about my standing before Him. Was I incredibly burdened by sin, or was I forgiven and justified? How could I tell? There was no sign. I could go straight to God, all right. No need for a priest (the thought would never have occurred to me). But all was silence. All I had were questions and doubts.

CAN YOU HEAR ME NOW?

When I discovered the Catholic Church, I was confronted for the first time with an answer to those questions, a solution to those doubts. That answer, of course, was the Sacrament of Reconciliation, which, I guess, was the sign I was looking for at age ten (and then some). Now, perhaps you might imagine that I ran gleefully into the first available confessional, waving a long list of wrongdoings in my hand. But I didn't. It all seemed a little too easy to me, and I think I retained a certain amount of suspicion.

I still didn't quite like the idea of airing my dirty linen in front of another person (the priest). All of us have a built-in aversion to sharing our faults and failings with another, and I was certainly no exception. Not only that, I guess I was still Protestant enough to question whether a priest's words of absolution would work the way I was told they would. The whole notion of Jesus granting authority to people — flawed human beings — to forgive sins in His name took some getting used to.

So I hemmed and hawed for a while, but one Saturday evening I decided to bite the bullet, gather all my courage, and go the whole Catholic distance. In other words, I decided to discover if God's mercy really was to be found within that little room that had always looked to me so much like a fancy broom closet.

I waited my turn (it was a disappointingly short wait, offering little time to reconsider and quietly slip away), and much too soon I was up. I took a deep breath, entered the confessional, and knelt down rather awkwardly, as the designer of that particular confessional seemed not to have considered the possibility of penitents who were over six feet tall. I had rehearsed the formula so often that I guess I just blurted it out: "Bless me, Father, for I have sinned." Okay, that part seemed to go all right. But now, I knew, came the hard part. I hesitated; then I hesitated some more. Then I actually did it, or perhaps it just happened. I actually began to name my sins, first slowly and uncomfortably, then with greater ease, and finally with a certain amount of gusto.

And when I was done, I heard them, the words of absolution with my own ears. I had read them before but never heard them, and they sounded like some of the most beautiful words anyone had ever spoken to me (and that's because they were):

> God, the Father of mercies,
> through the death and resurrection of his Son
> has reconciled the world to himself
> and sent the Holy Spirit among us
> for the forgiveness of sins;
> through the ministry of the Church

may God give you pardon and peace,
and I absolve you from your sins
in the name of the Father, and of the Son,
and of the Holy Spirit. (Rite of Penance, n. 46)

I left the confessional kind of in a daze. As I knelt in the church doing my penance, I kept hearing over and over again in my mind, "Pardon and peace" and "I absolve you." And guess what? I felt as if those words were true. I actually *felt* absolved. I felt as if I had received pardon. I actually felt something that I suspected might be peace.

In other words, I was blown away.

JESUS, I TRUST IN YOU

I'm still blown away, and I have come to love those words deeply. At times, I even long to hear them. Man is a sinful creature, and I am certainly no exception. I am every bit as conscious of my shortcomings as a Catholic as I was when I was a Protestant. In fact, I'm more conscious of them, for being forced to name my sins on a fairly regular basis makes me very cognizant of them and their sad repetition in my life. It can't help but give me a little humility.

Yet I no longer doubt that I am forgiven, and I'm not wasting my time looking for signs that God doesn't need to send me. I don't understand how it happened. It wasn't through an intellectual understanding of the Sacrament of Reconciliation alone, although that was probably part of it, but I believe in the depths of my soul that God uses this great sacrament to show His mercy in a unique way. After all, He created the sacrament to resonate with real people, flawed human beings like me who need to hear words of mercy being spoken.

The result for me was unexpected at first, but now I think I can depend on it: the lifting of an emotional weight that is bowing me down; the feeling of liberation that comes from being reconciled once again with our Father in heaven, of being made again into the person God wants me to be. I have often left the confessional, on my way to perform penances that pale in comparison to the gravity of my sins, with a huge smile on my face.

How blessed we are as Catholics to have this expression of God's infinite love for us. His mercy has often been described as "an ocean," and when I contemplate the Sacrament of Reconciliation, that's an image that often comes to my mind: an endless sea of mercy, inexhaustible and available to each one of us, gently washing away our sins. Another image that frequently comes to me has to do with water as well. It is that of a fountain that God causes to spring up in the midst of His Church to cleanse us of our sins — and not just cleanse us but strengthen us. Confession is a veritable fountain of graces to help us overcome the sin that plagues our lives.

I guess I just love confession, and I also guess that fact might make me part of a minority in the Church today. I know a number of cradle Catholics who have abandoned this wonderful sacrament, adopting an almost Protestant approach to things, one that almost seems to deny that Christ made the Church the conduit of His sacraments. It's an attitude that says: "It's just between God and me; I don't have to confess to a priest." That saddens me.

I have gained so much through this sacrament that it's almost painful for me to hear people disparage it. I know many people have had bad experiences in confession, and I don't doubt such stories; priests have certainly proved that they are as human and as sinful as the rest of us. But are those bad experiences really enough to make you want to cut yourself off from God's mercy, from His fountain of graces, His ocean of forgiveness?

The beauty of being Catholic is that if (when?) we stray from our faith, even if we've been away from the Church for years or even decades, *we're only one confession away from a state of grace.* That's a real gift. So I invite all converts and all cradle Catholics to join me in the confessional. (Not at the same time, of course!) Give yourself a chance to hear again those healing words of absolution. In other words, come on back in. The water in this ocean's a lot warmer than you think.

And if you're still looking for a sign, forget about the solar eclipse and the snowstorm in July: they're not going to happen. All you need to know is that Jesus endowed His Church with the ability to forgive any sin and that everything you're in search of can be found in a little room. You know the one. It looks sort of like a fancy broom closet ... and if you're not sure where to find it, try looking in the back of your church.

Chapter 10

Third Stumbling Block: The Mystical Body of Christ

And he put all things beneath his feet and gave him as head over all things to the church, which is his body, the fullness of the one who fills all things in every way.
— Ephesians 1:22-23

"Catholicism means you never have to be alone." That's a nice slogan, don't you think? I came up with it myself, and I'm kind of proud of it. In fact, I like it so much that I'm considering using it as a bumper sticker, giving those people in the SUV right behind me (the ones who lean on their horns the instant the light turns green) something to read and ponder as I leisurely press my foot down on the gas pedal.

But what do I mean by this kind of sweet-sounding and sentimental-seeming saying? Well, I don't mean anything sentimental at all. Those words simply state a fact and a very beautiful one at that. They also point out a rather marked difference between the Catholic Church and most of the Protestant world, one that many people might not fully appreciate. Let me explain.

As a Protestant, I understood my relationship with God to be very individual, a relationship that ultimately concerned nobody but me (and God, of course). To put it in its starkest terms, it was as if I stood alone before God, as if all that mattered were simply He and I. That can be a very beautiful place to be — alone in the presence of the Divine. But it can also be a very difficult place to be, for during our mortal lives our souls are always beset by some sort of turmoil, some kind of "fear and trembling." We are perpetually besieged by guilt and burdened with doubt. Let's face it: Ambiguity is our lot during every second of our mortal lives. And in such a state, the idea of being absolutely alone before God can be a little overwhelming, to say the least.

This radical individuality and aloneness before God had a profound effect on the way I used to view things, including the way I viewed the churches to which I belonged. Using this way of thinking, the supernatural dimension of the church was greatly diminished — so greatly diminished that it almost vanished. A church became little more than an association of like-minded Christians who hold similar beliefs and worship in the same manner. It was therefore potentially replaceable by another church if, for example, you came in conflict with your minister over some item of faith or if the central governing body of your denomination issued some declaration with which you strongly disagreed.

All this produced a kind of consumerist attitude toward faith. At a couple of different points, I shopped around for a church that suited my needs, one that appealed to me or left me with a satisfying emotional high on a Sunday morning. This meant that doctrines were downplayed. Sometimes they were so thoroughly replaced by feelings that the Christian life became based on the shifting sands of emotions rather than the bedrock of truth. In some cases, even the possibility of objective truth was rejected.

Mea culpa; mea culpa; mea culpa. Looking back, I shake my head in wonder. In our pre-Catholic period, Kathi and I bounced around from one denomination to another, sincerely looking for a "Bible-based" church but becoming exasperated when they all offered radically different views of Christianity — all based on different biblical interpretations! I now realize that what we were looking for during that period was not real truth; what we were after could almost be described as a good emotional fit, a place where we felt at home. It might sound harsh, but in a certain sense I wonder now if we were attempting to conform God to ourselves, rather than ourselves to God. You see, our understanding of things led us to believe that any group of Christians could comprise a bona fide "church" if they were sincere enough and worked at it hard enough.

That's about as far from the way the Catholic Church sees things as it's possible to get and still be on the same planet.

WHOSE CHURCH?

When I entered the Catholic Church, I discovered I was entering far more than just an organization of sincere Christians. I was entering something that had a life of its own — that pulsated with something infinitely transcending the combined lives of all its members. I was entering not simply an organization but a body — the Mystical Body of Christ — and I was entering it in a very literal way. The *Catechism* puts it like this:

> As Lord, Christ is also head of the Church, which is his Body (cf. Eph 1:22). Taken up to heaven and glorified after he had thus fully accomplished his mission, Christ dwells on earth

> in his Church. The redemption is the source of the authority that Christ, by virtue of the Holy Spirit, exercises over the Church. "The kingdom of God [is] already present in mystery," "on earth, the seed and the beginning of the kingdom" (LG 3; 5; cf. Eph 4:11-13). (n. 669)

Think about that for a minute: "Christ dwells on earth in his Church." That means that as members of the Church, each one of us is able to participate in Christ's life in His Church. And not only that: Through participating in this life, we are connected to each other in ways that we can barely fathom. We are, in fact, connected on the deepest of levels because we are not merely part of the same organization; we are part of the same *body*.

Frankly, I was bewildered by that idea when I first heard it. It seemed foreign and strange to me, and I wasn't sure I liked it very much. I also felt a little threatened by it. It seemed almost like one of those Hindu or Buddhist ideas to me: the ones that say the human soul is like a drop of water that flows into a divine ocean, thus continuing to exist as part of the whole while ceasing to exist in an individual way. I wasn't sure I could get on board with something like that.

Well, of course I didn't have to, for such a concept has nothing to do with the Catholic idea of the Mystical Body. Christ died on the cross not for humanity in general but for each and every one of us in our particularity. Would He then do anything to rob us of the very particularity for which He died? Of course not, and once I grasped that, I was on board. In fact I was on board with a vengeance.

This vision of the Church as a living body, a great web of connection, fills me with awe and also with a kind of hope, for through the Mystical Body of Christ I have become aware that I am part of a vast chorus of voices, an immense series of travelers on their way to the same destination. Christ's eternality sweeps away my solitude and overcomes the barrier of time. It brings me practically face-to-face with all those who have preceded me, with saints and martyrs both known and unknown. Through the Mystical Body of Christ, I am able to pray with the Fathers of the Church, to ask the intercession of great saints who went home to God centuries before I was born, to live with them as if they were present — for they *are* present through the Mystical Body of Christ. They are present to me and to you.

WE'RE NEVER ALONE

For this reason, I know I am no longer alone and trembling before God, and what's even more important, I know I don't have to rely on my own power any longer. I can ask the saints for their help when I am tempted, for their prayers when I am distraught, or simply for their presence when I am lonely, for I now understand that they are not merely historical figures to be emulated but companions along the way, helpers — the ones I can depend on most fully. In the Body of Christ, I am never alone. I have the support of — I am buoyed up by — an unseen multitude too vast to be counted.

Yet despite the great beauty of the Church's understanding of the Body of Christ and the great consolation that it should give us, I often find myself wondering how many people really appreciate this great wonder that is ours through Christ. More than a few Catholics have acquired the same consumerist mentality of which I have already spoken, embracing the idea that a church should make us feel a certain way, should satisfy what we think our spiritual needs of the moment are. To put it bluntly, some Catholics approach the Church as if it were a spiritual supply store where they can come and go, "purchasing" what they need whenever their cupboards are empty.

Perhaps some of this is the result of the recent, devastating clergy scandals in which the Church and some of her representatives fell so far short of what they were called to do and to be. Perhaps because of this, the institutional Church has appeared to be untrustworthy, making some want to step outside it and try to establish that kind of individual relationship with God of which I spoke earlier. I understand that temptation — I *really* do — but I also understand its faults and its failings. It is the Protestant impulse, a turning away from that vast web of connection that is the Mystical Body of Christ and a turning toward an idea of aloneness before God, of having no one to rely on but oneself as one stands in "fear and trembling" before the Divine.

I've been there, and it's a very dramatic place to be. But I would never go back there because I've found the place for which I was made, as one of that vast chorus of voices all praising God as we slowly make our journey toward Him, as a member of a body that transcends time and place, the Mystical Body of Christ.

It's a really good place to be, and it's the place where you never have to be alone.

Chapter 11

Fourth Stumbling Block: Mary

"My soul proclaims the greatness of the Lord;
  my spirit rejoices in God my savior.
For he has looked upon his handmaid's lowliness;
  behold, from now on will all ages call me blessed."
                                    — Luke 1:46-48

Let's imagine a discussion between two Christian friends. One is an evangelical Protestant (we'll call him Jeffrey), and the other is a Catholic (we'll call him Patrick). The two of them like to talk about all sorts of things in lengthy, free-wheeling conversations.

One day, in the midst of such a dialogue, Patrick asks Jeffrey the following question: "Who do *you* think Mary is?" Jeffrey is quick to respond and says, "Mary is the humble woman of Nazareth who, in her obedience and faith, made possible the incarnation of Jesus."

He is quietly proud of the elegant succinctness of his answer. But he's not just proud; he's also puzzled. That's because, although Patrick is nodding in agreement, he's still looking expectantly at Jeffrey.

"And?" Patrick says, his words an obvious prompt.

"And what?" Jeffrey responds.

"And what about the rest?"

By now, Jeffrey is confused.

"What rest? There is no rest. Who do you think Mary is?" he asks, noting that his friend appears dissatisfied.

Patrick takes a deep breath before answering (he has to, because he has a lot to say): "Mary is the Mother of God; she is the Theotokos; she is the Immaculate Conception; she is Our Lady of Perpetual Help; she is the Mediatrix of all Graces."

Now it's Jeffrey's turn to be shocked. He knows his Bible well, and a line from it — flashing like a warning sign — leaps into his mind: "There is one God, and one mediator between God and men, the man Christ Jesus" (1 Timothy 2:5, KJV).

Jeffrey is about to demand an explanation of this "mediatrix" thing but finds he can't because his friend is on a roll. You see, Patrick has suddenly recalled the Litany of Loreto, which he used to recite as a schoolboy, and he's decided the time is right to recite some of it again, at least the parts he can remember: "Mary is the Mother of the Church; she is the Virgin most powerful; she is the Virgin most merciful; she is the mirror of justice; she is the cause of our joy; she is the mystical rose; she is the comforter of the afflicted; she is the morning star; she is the ark of the covenant."

Jeffrey has no clue as to what's going on. How can Mary be the ark of the covenant? The ark of the covenant was some kind of box with the Ten Commandments in it that the Israelites carried around in the desert for forty years. Again he tries to protest, but again he can't get a word in edgewise. Then Patrick finally does it. He crosses the line and ends his list of Marian titles in a way that might possibly also end their friendship. "Mary is Queen of heaven and earth," he proclaims, looking rather proud of himself. A long hush ensues before a shocked Jeffrey begins to sputter: "That's ... that's ... that's ... that's not just heresy. That's idolatry!"

And that's a big problem, for the devotion that Catholics and Orthodox Christians show to Mary the Mother of God on a regular basis is so foreign to much of the Protestant world that it doesn't even look Christian to them. It really does look like idolatry, like a reversion to a kind of polytheism. As such, it seems not only wrong but deeply sinful because it seems to divert worship from the only One who should truly receive it — in other words, from God Himself.

A MOTHER'S PRAYER

A large part of this problem that Protestants have in understanding Mary can, I think, be traced to a rather unlikely source: the fact that the Protestant and Catholic ideas of prayer are actually somewhat different. Catholicism contains the entire understanding of prayer that exists in the Protestant world, but it goes beyond it, meaning that the Catholic idea is more expansive and inclusive. For most Protestants, prayer exists simply between a human soul and God. It's a two-way street: You pray to God and God responds as God wills.

For a Catholic, there is much more to prayer than that. Our participation in the Mystical Body of Christ makes possible an intimate connection with the saints in heaven, and through this connection God permits us to be in prayerful relationship with those saints. This is especially true in the case of Mary, the Mother of God. Thus, for a Catholic, prayer is not a two-way street but countless streets and avenues that we can venture down. We don't need a map because we have friends on all these streets, and each one of those friends will point us toward our ultimate destination — God. We can and do pray to saints and especially to the Mother of God. Yet no Catholic sees that prayer as the same as one he would make to God. It is not completely unrelated, yet it is radically different.

Prayer to Our Lady is a cry to both a friend and a mother. She is a mother who knew suffering and love, having experienced both during her earthly life. But she has been drawn up into the heart of love, into the heart of God, and so we pray "through" her to Him. In the Catholic understanding, Mary is like a pane of perfectly clear glass. As light reaches the glass and flows through it, so our prayers reach the Mother of God and flow through her to her Son. Thus, for a Catholic, prayer to Mary never stops with her. Prayer to Mary is ultimately prayer to Christ. And in a very real sense, she perfects these prayers.

We do not ask her for miracles, for no one but God can perform one. We do not ask her to change our lives, for only God can do that. We ask only that she carry our prayer to her Divine Son, to the Holy Trinity, to the heart of God, and that she pray for and with us — that she add her prayers (the prayers of a human being in whom no trace of estrangement from God exists) to our frail and feeble prayers.

Now, I get how strange this sounds to evangelical ears. During my days at Steubenville, you might remember that a good friend named Carol told me exactly what I have just written. In fact, she told me many times, and was incredibly patient, as she explained the difference between praying to God and praying through Mary or one of the saints. Yet none of it made any sense to me back then, and it took years before it did. Now, however, it seems not just normal or reasonable but an indisputable reality that has profoundly enriched my spiritual life.

HUMILITY AND OBEDIENCE

When I was a Protestant, I believed just as Jeffrey does that Mary was "the humble woman of Nazareth who, in her obedience and faith, made possible the incarnation of Jesus." I still believe that today, but now that I am a Catholic I see there is more to Mary than that — that there *had to be* more to Mary than that. For example, I believe she was created to be unique because her role in our redemption was unique.

In other words, Mary was not just one of a multitude of potential candidates for that job. It was not as if the angel Gabriel was wandering from one Jewish town to another looking for a young woman to take him up on a very strange offer. He sure wasn't going around talking to himself like this: "Okay. Ruth declined, so did Sarah and Leah. Rebecca wouldn't even open the door. The jury's still out on Naomi, but it doesn't look good. Who's next on the list? Oh yeah, there's a kid named Mary on the next block. She's kind of young and the shy type, but as long as I'm in the neighborhood I guess I may as well drop in and ask."

No! Mary was in the mind of God from before time began. She is a part of God's creation that soared (and continues to soar) above the rest. Remember that she is called the New Eve, indicating that she participates in that state of human perfection that existed before the Fall — before sin entered human life. She had to be perfectly pure, to be unburdened by the many frailties that are the legacy of sin, for she was destined to contain within her the infinity of God, an infinity that the whole universe cannot hope to contain.

Mary was the chosen vessel through whom hope and life were brought into a world mired in despair and death. She alone could have the courage to say yes to God because she alone was not estranged from God by sin of any kind. She was the only one who could stand by the cross in utter heartbreak but unshaken faith. Ruth and Leah and Sarah and all the rest, good and pious Jewish girls as they probably were, just wouldn't have been up to the job.

The Protestant world mistakes our veneration of Mary for worship and believes it to be an incursion of paganism deep into the Christian soul. I once felt like that myself, but I've learned a lot since those days. Scott Hahn gave a talk many years ago in which he asked a provocative question. It went something like this: If you were God and you were planning on the Incarnation, wouldn't you make the mother of the Second Person of the Holy Trinity different from other mothers, more perfect, more holy? I had to admit that if I were God, I probably would do all those things. That question started me thinking that maybe the Catholic Church wasn't so far off the mark when it came to the Mother of God.

Some time later, when I met Scott and he gave me a rosary, I wasn't even sure what a rosary was, let alone how to use one. But I learned. I can't explain it, but as I tried to pray that prayer on those beads, I met someone — not right off the bat but eventually. The person I met was not God, but one who could show me God, who could take me to God. I still pray the Rosary as often as I can, and I still know that person. She is not God, but she still carries me to God.

JUST THE FACTS, MOM

Let's face facts: Nobody's ever met a Catholic who would say he worships Mary, who imagines that she is in any sense divine. I would even go beyond that and say that the Church wouldn't have the faintest idea what to do with her as divine — as a goddess. Like the rest of Christianity (and the rest of the monotheistic religions), the Catholic Church divides all that is into two categories: God and God's creation. There's no room in that division for another divine or even quasi-divine being. We've got God. That's it.

Yes, we do call her the Queen of heaven, just as our friend Patrick did. Yet no Catholic believes that in saying that he's putting Mary on a par with Jesus. Jesus is the King of heaven and earth; He reigns and rules eternally. Yet as the mother of Jesus and the Mother of God, why shouldn't Mary be considered a queen? In countries that still have monarchies, isn't the wife of the reigning king called a queen? Isn't the mother of the king called the queen mother? Mary neither reigns nor rules in the way her Divine Son does, but she shares in his kingship as a queen mother, for she is totally united with her Son.

Not only that, just check out the Book of Revelation sometime. There, in chapter 12, we read about "a woman clothed with the sun, with the moon under her feet, and on her head a crown of twelve stars." She's about to give birth to "a male child, destined to rule all the nations with an iron rod" (12:1, 5). If that's not a queen, then I don't know what a queen is; and if you can't see that as an image of the Mother of God, then I suggest you reread the text a few times — slowly, and making a real effort to bracket your preconceptions.

Catholics don't want Mary to be a goddess, and we definitely don't want her to become an idol for us. We just want her to be what God created her to be: a mother — our mother. We want her to be the mother who will always pray for us, who in a sense perfects our prayers, the one whose prayers become a channel of God's grace to us. And this is what a Catholic really means when he calls Mary the Mediatrix of Grace. It is not that she is a source of grace, for only God could be that. As salvation came into the world through Mary, so grace enters the world through her as well. She never competes with her Divine Son and certainly never equals Him. But through her intimate, humble, and eternal union with Him, she becomes the perfect conduit, not only of our prayers to Christ but of God's grace to our fallen world. She is forever the instrument through which God's love flows.

And if you're not Catholic and managed to get through all that without needing smelling salts, you might actually be a *closet* Catholic … whether you know it or not.

Chapter 12

Fifth Stumbling Block: Faith vs. Works

For just as a body without a spirit is dead, so also faith without works is dead.

— James 2:26

When did the Protestant Reformation begin? Most people date it to October 31, 1517, when Martin Luther nailed his Ninety-Five Theses to the door of All Saints Church in Wittenberg, Germany. When I was a Protestant, that was a day not just to recall with pride but to celebrate; it was a day when we imagined the Church had been reborn or at least had been restored to what it should have been all along. What a difference a change of perspective can make! Now that I'm a Catholic, I see that day more as a time of mourning, a day when something that was whole began to shatter. It is the moment when a huge part the Church embarked on a journey to become merely "churches."

In the nearly five centuries since then, the world has changed radically. Yet this sad division has not changed. It grows and persists, and by its growth and persistence it weakens all of Christianity, making the Christian witness to the world appear confused and contradictory — and easier to reject.

Let me give you a couple of personal examples. I went to a Pentecostal school from grades eight to ten. I liked it there, but the place made me worry about my ultimate fate. Why? Because I couldn't pray in tongues — and let me tell you, it wasn't from any lack of trying, but how could I be expected to pray in tongues when I had trouble praying in English? My Pentecostal friends understand praying in tongues as baptism in the Holy Spirit: the sign God gives when He saves you and makes you His own. Without it your fate remains uncertain, to say the least.

My Baptist friends, on the other hand, didn't worry much about things like that; their approach was simpler and less theatrical — certainly less verbal. According to them, all you had to do to be saved was to accept Jesus as your personal Lord and Savior. That sounded better to me; unlike praying in tongues, it seemed like something I could manage, so I gave it a try — actually I gave it several tries — but something always seemed wrong. I never felt what I assumed I was supposed to feel, never felt a dramatic change in my relationship with God, never felt the clouds break apart, letting the light of divine redemption suddenly shine on me in all its staggering brilliance.

By the time I left that school, I was very confused as to which approach was right (maybe neither was!). I was also beginning to wonder if I really had the knack for being a Christian, as I never got the results that Christians were supposed to get when I did the things that Christians were supposed to do.

This sort of confusion wasn't limited to one Canadian kid. It's common, and it's a big problem. The myriad divisions within Christianity have created different and competing understandings of many things, even of such basic notions as how salvation is brought into being by God. Profound theological disagreements began in the Reformation, and despite the great efforts of many fine Christians on both sides of the divide, those disagreements remain. We Christians don't burn each other at the stake any longer — which is an undeniable step in the right direction — but we sometimes still find ourselves diametrically opposed on some pretty basic issues. These issues can become major stumbling blocks for the convert.

For the Protestant, entering the Catholic Church involves adopting a new way of seeing the Divine-human relationship. This can be disorienting, and it can also seem to require an abandonment of ideas so deeply held that they almost seem like part of our DNA. That's not just frightening; it can be terrifying. It's like the ground is suddenly disintegrating beneath your feet.

"EITHER/OR" AND/OR "BOTH/AND"?

One such issue is that of faith versus works. As far as I know, we've been arguing about this one since the moment Martin Luther hammered his first nail into that church door. Yet when you get right down to it, it's not really a confusing issue. I think it boils down to this: Are we so far gone as sinners that we can do nothing for ourselves — can participate in no way in our own salvation — or do we have certain capabilities to respond to the grace that God gives us? The answers to this question show how differently Catholicism and Protestantism see both the human being and the Divine-human relationship.

The traditional Protestant approach says we're pretty much passive recipients of God's grace. We can do nothing beyond making an act of faith in Jesus Christ, like the one my Baptist friends encouraged me to make; after that, our job is simply to maintain our faith. God takes care of the rest. Works aren't an essential part of the deal. In the Protestant view, it is as if we are carried along by God as a leaf might be carried along by a stream into which it has fallen.

The traditional Catholic response to this question says something quite different: Although we may be heavily burdened by sin, we're definitely not so far gone that our acts, our works, are meaningless in the grand scheme of things. I guess you can say that, for the Catholic, there's no free Divine ride; the initial act of faith is necessary, of course, but it's just the beginning of the story. We're in a partnership, and we're expected to pull our weight. We're not that leaf in the stream. We're in the stream all right, and we're being propelled along by the current, but we're still expected to try to swim in the right direction.

The Presbyterianism of my childhood unsurprisingly put great emphasis on personal faith rather than works. What an individual believed was of primary importance. What he did was clearly secondary. And because that is what I learned and what everyone around me took for granted, I assumed it made perfect sense. It was, in fact, the way I understood things for years. Perhaps it's even the way I understood things during my first years as a Catholic — at least to some extent. Old habits die hard. Like many Protestants, I thought such an idea simply acknowledged God as God really is: ultimate Sovereign of everything. It admitted the truth: that we are completely dependent on Him, that we can do nothing on our own, that heaven is not within our puny grasp. Salvation is an unmerited gift, not our due.

In other words, I just didn't get the Catholic Church's emphasis on works. I thought that such an emphasis meant that Catholics were being presumptuous, almost trying to usurp the place of God or at least not being humble enough before Him. I imagined they thought they could get to heaven on their own, just by doing enough of the right things, by observing all the rules (and they had so many!). It seemed almost pharisaical to me, or at least it seemed the sort of things that I imagined Pharisees would do if there were still Pharisees. I thought that Catholics, by their emphasis on works, were trying to reinstitute the kind of complex law, with its rewards and punishments, that had characterized the Judaism of Jesus' time. Didn't Paul tell us that we were done with that sort of thing?

It was a long time before I realized I was looking at this problem in the wrong way. Over the years, I came to see that the view that predominates in Protestantism (and was probably inherited directly from Luther himself) is a view that sometimes unnecessarily splits things in two that should remain one. In other words, things are generally understood in an either/or sort of way: either faith or works, as if the two were somehow mutually exclusive. I had completely imbibed this approach. It was, as far as I was concerned, simply the way God did business. Even when I would read the Epistle of St. James — an epistle Luther despised and wanted deleted from the Bible — and would come to the words "faith without works is dead" (2:16), it just didn't sink in.

But then one day it did.

I can't give you a date when it happened. All I know is that it did happen. As I became more immersed in the study and the living out of Catholicism, I began to see this either/or division as being less necessary than I had supposed — than Protestantism supposes. I began to see the possibility of both/and. Gradually, the faith-versus-works problem solved itself for me — or perhaps I should say, it revealed itself to be a non-issue.

SAINTLY SOLUTIONS

As I became more Catholic in my way of looking at things, I began to understand that there can be no conflict between faith and works because the two are intimately and inextricably bound together — two sides of the same coin. Real faith doesn't think about works and decide which of them to perform. It doesn't weigh which act will increase one's reservoir of merit in God's supposed savings bank. Real faith overflows into works, much as a spring bubbling up from deep in the earth overflows onto the ground around it.

If I have real faith, I should see the image of God reflected in every person I meet. If some of those people are in need, how can I, as a man of faith, stand by idly? I can't. My faith must overflow into works of charity — of love. If there is no such overflow, if faith remains a hermetically sealed relationship between God and me, then something is very wrong.

As the years progressed, I began to understand this in a clearer way. The study of the saints, especially St. Thérèse of Lisieux, helped. She showed me that as your faith grows, so do your works, that the imitation of Christ means constantly learning how to deepen the gift of self to others, that the life of faith and the life of self-giving are identical and can never be split apart.

All this, once I realized it, gave me a foundation on which to build. It didn't really destroy my Protestant conception of faith, as I once feared it might. I learned not to split apart what is meant to remain together, and in the process I learned that the faith I had grown up with didn't need to be abandoned, but rather expanded and fulfilled. In other words, the ground stopped disintegrating beneath my feet. Instead, it became more solid than ever.

When it comes to explaining the Catholic idea of the relationship between faith and works, I don't think I can do much better than to quote St. Josemaría Escrivá, the founder of Opus Dei. So I think I'll give him the last word:

> I assure you, my children, that when a Christian carries out with love the most insignificant everyday action, that action overflows with the transcendence of God. That is why I have told you so often, and hammered away at it, that the Christian vocation consists in making heroic verse out of the prose of each day. Heaven and earth seem to merge, my children, on the horizon. But where they really meet is in your hearts, when you sanctify your everyday lives…. (St. Josemaría Escrivá, homily titled "Passionately Loving the World")

Chapter 13

Sixth Stumbling Block: Authority

And so I say to you, you are Peter, and upon this rock I will build my church, and the gates of the netherworld shall not prevail against it.

— Matthew 16:18

I've already mentioned more than once that the lack of an ultimate authority in Protestantism was a big problem for me. When the Protestant faith was born in the sixteenth century, it was based on a number of things, but one of the most important was the idea that all authority could be located in the biblical text. The corollary to this was that the meaning of that text could be discerned by all those who approached it with sincerity, prayerfulness, and a reasonable amount of intelligence.

At least, that was Luther's idea as I understand it. *Sola scriptura* was the Latin term that expressed that idea. In a nutshell, it means "Scripture alone" is the entire source of doctrine. Oddly enough, this idea is found nowhere in the Bible, so the doctrine that says all doctrines must find their source in Scripture does not itself find its source in Scripture ... which is something that always puzzled me.

And that's not the only thing that puzzled me. If the true interpretation of Scripture is achievable by any sincere and prayerful Christian, then why would there be thousands of Protestant denominations with differing scriptural interpretations? That fact indicated a real problem to me, and as an illustration of the problem, I have come up with the following little story, which I call "Martin's Awful Nightmare." Hope you enjoy it.

It's a rainy November day in Germany. The date is the tenth of the month, and the year is 1533, which means it is the fiftieth birthday of the great Protestant reformer Martin Luther. Martin's birthday party has just ended and the last guests have departed. Not only has Martin had a great time, he's stuffed to the gills with ice cream and cake (black forest, of course) and perhaps just a drop too much Riesling. The birthday boy has made out like a bandit, and the place is littered with gifts.

One of them is especially intriguing to our intrepid reformer and so rare in Germany during the sixteenth century that it may even be unique: a time machine. Thrilled by this astonishing gift, Martin can't wait to use it. So, being the pro-active kind of guy he is (remember those Ninety-Five Theses), he decides to make an impromptu visit to the early twenty-first century just for the heck of it.

Time Lapse

Martin enters the time machine, presses some buttons and the contraption sputters, quivers, shakes, and then stops. Opening the door, he cautiously emerges.

The world is different and disorienting — the time machine seems to have worked — but in the distance Martin sees something familiar: a building with a steeple and a cross on top — a church. Martin rushes up to it and enters.

He's had the good luck to land in the twentieth-first century on a Sunday morning, and there's a service in progress. Martin listens to the sermon eagerly but is astonished to discover that the topic involves something he's never heard of — something called the Rapture.

Dumbfounded, he listens to the preacher go on and on about the people who will be left behind and those who will be saved at the Second Coming of Christ. It seems to bear no relationship to the Christianity Martin has known his whole life. But what is more incomprehensible is the way the preacher is justifying his words by referring to a biblical text from the Book of Revelation. "The Rapture is coming, and the Bible proves it," thunders the preacher in conclusion. That's just too much for Martin. He hightails it out of that church.

Discovering a small, unassuming chapel across the street, he enters it and finds another service in progress. But what kind of service can it be? There is no music, no sermon, no prayers, no bread, no wine, no nothing. The congregants simply sit motionless.

Impatient by nature, Martin turns to the woman next to him. "What are they waiting for?" he demands. "Why don't they get on with it?"

"They're waiting for the inner light," she whispers back.

"The what?" Martin demands.

"The inner light," the woman repeats. "We're Quakers." The woman turns out to be the helpful sort. Opening a Bible to John 8:12, she reads very softly: 'I am the light of the world: he that followeth me shall not walk in darkness, but shall have the light of life' (KJV). See, the Bible says the inner light is within us all. We just have to wait patiently for it to manifest itself."

"Madame, your exegesis is in serious error. That is not what that verse means," Martin states so loudly that everyone in the room stares at him. Martin storms out of the chapel convinced that the twenty-first century could greatly benefit from the burning of a few heretics.

There is yet another church on the street. But is it a church? It looks like one, but the sign in front calls it a Kingdom Hall and the people within call themselves Jehovah's Witnesses. What can this mean? Martin is mystified but intrigued. He enters in search of sanity. Unfortunately, he's disappointed.

A man, whom the others call an elder, is giving a talk, and Martin listens intently. "Blood transfusions are unbiblical. In fact, they are sinful. The Bible teaches this clearly," declares the man, quoting two verses from the Book of Leviticus.

Martin, who has struggled with anger-management issues his entire life, has had it. He leaps to his feet. "You are not only wrong, sir, you are also a heretic and should be bound over for trial! Those verses refer only to the eating of blood. They form part of the Mosaic code, which has been abolished by our Divine Savior. You lead your flock astray, sir. Faith alone saves. Blood has no —" But that's as far as he gets. Martin is physically ejected from the church and deposited rather roughly on his backside on the lawn.

Picking himself up, he trudges on, visiting one church after another. In the next one, people sing and dance and babble meaninglessly — or at least it seems meaningless to Martin, who suggests that the assistance of a physician might not be out of order. He is quickly told that these babblers are not ill but in the grip of the Holy Spirit. He is also informed that speaking in tongues is a vital part of Christianity, and that the Bible states that plainly. A man starts quoting Bible verses from the Book of Acts and the First Letter to the Corinthians at Martin, who decides he has entered a den of madmen.

Again he rushes down the street and into another church. In this one, he discovers people handling serpents — serpents that are alive and don't look very happy. As Martin runs for his life, he is told that such a practice is authentically Christian and that the warrant for it can be easily discovered by anyone who cares to look in the Gospel of Mark.

A perceptive guy, Martin has come to the conclusion that the entire twenty-first century has gone bonkers and worries that if he doesn't leave soon he, too, may go off the deep end. Yearning for his time machine and the clarity of the sixteenth century, he dashes down the street.

This is the worst birthday ever! It's dawned on Martin that his precious doctrine of *sola scriptura* might have a few weaknesses he hadn't anticipated, and this disturbs him. He's also started muttering to himself, which makes people avoid eye contact with him on the street. "I've got to get back to the drawing board on this one," he says, as he jumps into the time machine and heads home to the sixteenth century. "I've got some major revising to do."

Within seconds Martin is home. He falls exhausted onto his couch, but when he awakes he remembers nothing of the future that shocked him to the core — the time machine apparently suppresses memories. Instead, he recalls only that he had too much cake and too much wine, which seem to have conspired to give him a nightmare of sorts, one that he can't quite summon to mind but had something to do with running from church to church. He shrugs and then remembers that he must prepare a sermon to deliver on Sunday. Its topic is one of his favorites: the unquestionable authority of the biblical text and the ability of all sincere Christians to interpret it for themselves. He smiles. Then he picks up his quill pen, dips it into his inkwell, and begins writing.

⁓

So that's my story, and you're right: It's over the top and not entirely fair. But I think it makes my point that the biblical text alone cannot be an absolute authority because it can be interpreted in many different and sometimes bizarre ways.

HABEMUS PAPAM

What the Christian world needs is a living authority, one that does not lie inert on a page but can explain itself, that can clarify things when clarity is needed. In other words, it needs something — or, rather, someone — sort of like … well, you know … sort of like — brace yourself, because here it comes! — sort of like … the … pope.

There, I said it. And I meant it. And, by the way, this is something I once thought I could never bring myself to say, but now I can, and I can do it easily.

The Church needs stability. It needs an immovable rock upon which to stand. It needs to know what is truly Christian and what is not, for many things appear to be Christian on the outside but turn out to be something very different when you get to their essence. I am reminded of my days at Steubenville when I assumed that the use of birth control involved no moral dimension at all. It was reading *Humanae Vitae* that changed my mind and opened my eyes. *Humanae Vitae* expresses the love that is found at the heart of Christianity. Yet I could never have derived the ideas put forth in that document from reading Scripture alone. I never heard those ideas expressed by any major Protestant body.

When I recall reading that document, I recall reading something that spoke with a strange kind of authority, an authority that was difficult to deny. And it was an authority that I liked, one that seemed to put me on solid ground. But where did this authority come from?

For a long time, I hesitated on the whole pope question. I tried to figure a way to become Catholic without the pope. If anyone else is thinking along those lines, I'm here to say: Don't bother; it can't be done.

What eventually helped me see the pope as final arbiter, as source of authority, was actually a twist on the question that Scott Hahn once asked regarding Mary — the one that was the key for my understanding of the Catholic Church's Marian teachings. Extrapolating from Scott's Marian question, I came up with this: If God wanted His Church to continue beyond the deaths of the original disciples, wouldn't he have created a structure for it to do so and a voice of authority that could deal with problems as they arose — a structure and a voice that would remain consistent over the centuries and not be swayed by changing fashions?

If you answer that one in the affirmative — and you really have to unless you imagine God to be rather thoughtless and slapdash — you have to ask what that voice of authority might be. It can't be Scripture alone, as I have attempted to demonstrate in "Martin's Awful Nightmare." Another reason it can't be Scripture is that the Church didn't finish establishing the biblical canon until the fifth century (the four hundreds), and so what did those people who lived and died before that point do?

The only candidate remaining for "voice of authority" is the Church itself. So how about ecumenical councils like the ones the early Church called to iron out theological difficulties? Fine. They spoke with the authority that was needed, but I think we all have to admit they're a little unwieldy. You can't just call a council every time somebody has a good question or every time a dispute — or even a crisis — arises. So that answer might be partially right but won't work in the long run.

What's left? Not much that I can see except the guy in the white cassock — you know, the one who occupies the See of Peter, the same Peter who Jesus called the rock, the one to whom He gave the keys to the Kingdom. Yes, that guy.

So if God wanted His Church to operate well and truly bring people to Christ, He would have created a center of authority that could operate efficiently and clearly: one that could pull people back, over and over again, when they started handling snakes, or talking about the Rapture, or marrying their cats, or any of the thousand other things Christians might be persuaded to do. In other words, God would have given the Church something like the pope, and since the pope is just one person and can't be everywhere at the same time, mightn't God have created a structure that involved other people united with the pope — you know, kind of like bishops in apostolic succession?

I don't know about you, but I have no trouble thinking that God is smart enough to come up with ideas like that. The pope and the bishops united with him form the most logical structure for preserving the essence of Christianity. Words on a page can't do it, and ad hoc committees can't do it — at least not over long periods of time. We've got to have a pope — a voice that can speak clearly and consistently. Without one, we're only a step or two away from "Martin's Awful Nightmare."

Chapter 14

Seventh Stumbling Block: The Church's Imperfections

"Master, to whom shall we go? You have the words of eternal life."

— John 6:68

People reject the Catholic Church for many reasons, and some of these are more understandable than others. I hate to say it, but the most understandable one at the moment is also probably one of the most powerful ones in our culture. It's also the one that has hurt countless people, whether directly or indirectly.

I'm talking here about the priestly sex abuse scandal that seemed to simmer its way through the 1990s and really erupted in an overwhelming way in 2002 and 2003. There's no way around it: Some priests (as well as members of religious orders, but we'll speak here primarily of priests) were guilty of atrocious crimes — and in certain cases, the problems were mishandled by bishops. There have been no winners in this crisis, just a long list of losers. Only God knows the full extent of havoc that has resulted.

Public perception of the Church after the scandal broke is very different from what it was before. The Catholic Church, once highly regarded in our country, became an object of suspicion and sometimes even of derision as a direct result. It seemed, at least to some, that the Church was shown to preach one thing and practice something absolutely contrary. The scandal has weakened the Church's voice in all areas related to morality, especially to sexual morality. In some circles, the Church is now perceived as a fatally flawed institution or even the utterly corrupt and morally bankrupt institution that certain fundamentalist bodies have always claimed it to be.

The Church is going to need another fifty years just to begin to recover from this self-inflicted wound.

So what to do in the meantime?

SLOW HEALING

For me, the most important thing to do is to recall a number of very different but related points. One is that sin by its very nature always leads to pain. It also has ripple effects, because even sins that seem to be "private" really aren't. Serious sin should remind us — as nothing else does — of our need for Christ and His mercy in our lives. It is only through Him that the problem of sin can effectively be addressed. Yet as members of His body, we know that we have a part to play in the healing of sin. It just goes with the territory. Perhaps all we can do is walk alongside those who have been wounded, offering our friendship, presence, and prayers. But who knows what value that may have? It could be incalculable.

We are all capable of failure, even spectacularly so. None of us hovers like an angel above the earthly struggle, so none of us should be quick to condemn others when they fail — even if they fail in a big way. Perhaps we have avoided serious sin for years or even decades. Wonderful! But tomorrow's story has yet to be written. When it is, would it really be impossible that it might include something about us suddenly and inexplicably failing? Okay, I know what you're thinking, and I agree: Most of us would fail in a very different way from that of the priests who have caused such immense suffering. But can we really say that it is impossible for us to fail and to fail spectacularly?

To be a Christian is to know that we deal with the effects of original sin every day. Each one of us is in almost constant inner conflict. Not to put too fine a point on it, we are at war with our own powerful (and only partially understood) yearnings and impulses. That war lasts a lifetime. Who among us can really say he has completely mastered greed, pride, anger, lust, or any of the other Seven Deadly Sins? I'm here to tell you right now, I'm not even close.

So that constitutes the first point I try to remember. The second is this: The Church is not identical with her institutions and her personnel. She infinitely transcends all that we are able to see of her because she is ultimately the Mystical Body of Christ. She is not the priest in your local parish or even your bishop, and certainly not the church buildings or schools. All those people and things are part of the Church in one way or another, of course, but they are not her essence.

That means that the Church isn't defined by the sins of her members — as egregious as some of those sins have been. Rather, she's defined by the Lordship of Jesus Christ, whose mercy we all need. We will always be a Church of sinners. What's important is to continue to strive for sanctity, even when we fail. By God's grace, even our sins — for we all share in a sinful nature — can be transformed and used for good, if we are willing to cooperate.

It's also important to recall, and perhaps to meditate upon, the fact that a moment of wickedness and betrayal was actually part and parcel of the birth of the Church. Judas betrayed Jesus on the very evening of the first Eucharist, only a short time after he had received the Eucharistic Christ into his heart and soul for the first (and obviously last) time. Judas was given the gift of life, of infinite love with no strings attached. He rejected it utterly — and with a kiss of all things! Thus he transformed — or, perhaps, deformed — a sign of love into a symbol of terrible betrayal. He made a mockery of love and turned away from life to run toward death. It was a betrayal of almost incomprehensible dimensions, yet its wickedness did not swallow up the rest. On the contrary, the very mechanism of death that Judas set into motion was transformed into its opposite. From it flowed and continues to flow a life and a love so powerful that it could not be stopped by even the greatest wickedness — a life and love that could not be overcome by any betrayal.

So we, like the One we follow, have been betrayed. However, we have been given the tools to move forward and the hope that somehow, even out of wickedness and betrayal, something new will be born.

The next important point to remember is that although the scope of the scandal seemed to overwhelm us, it really involved a small percentage of priests. Just as eleven of the apostles remained after Judas' betrayal, so the vast majority of priests were in no way guilty of wrongdoing. Most of them were trying their best despite the adverse circumstances. Most of them were doing pretty well.

It is helpful to recall that the work of the Church has gone on for centuries and has produced great good in spite of having some scoundrel popes, heretic priests, and corrupt members. Think of the faithful priests and religious, who, from the earliest days of the Church, have made God's love manifest in our troubled world. Think of those like Mother Teresa of Calcutta or Father Damian of Molokai, who cared for the sick, fed the hungry, helped the poor, educated children, and gave hope to the dying. That saintly work stands firm, undiminished by the sinful actions of others, and the Church carries on similar saintly work today as its members serve the needy and all those on "the peripheries," as Pope Francis says.

So, did the scandal affect me in any way? You can bet it did, like few things have ever done. Did it make me regret my conversion? No. I have gained too much from the Catholic Church. I have experienced God's power and God's healing through her too many times. Why should I leave, and where else could I go?

Christ brought me into the Church, and that is where I will stay. I know that the Church, being full of sinners, will disappoint me from time to time. It might even crush me now and again. But I'm not budging. I've learned to look beyond all that, beyond the Church's faults and frailties, even of clergy and religious, to the Mystical Body of Christ, to the Blessed Mother and the saints, to the One who never betrays and never hurts, to the One who comes to me when I approach the altar.

And that's not just good enough for me: that's infinitely more than I could ask or imagine.

Chapter 15

The Worst Stumbling Block of All: Me

What I do, I do not understand. For I do not do what I want, but I do what I hate.

— Romans 7:15

Well, I've gone on for over a hundred pages about how great the Catholic Church is, so here's my question: If all that I said is true (which it is), why aren't people flocking to the Church? Why, instead, are her numbers dwindling, as young people drift away in large numbers, as countless souls depart in seeming indifference?

I suppose there are many answers to that question, but here's one that a businessman like me would be likely to focus on: branding.

Let me explain. If the Church were a corporation, we would not hesitate to say that she had a "branding" problem. Her products — the sacraments — are unique, but they've been around for a long time, and her market has become a "mature" one (just think of all that gray hair you see at Sunday Mass). The Church doesn't have the pizzazz or freshness to attract the young in a culture that thrives on novelty and values newness over depth. She seems to speak of a world of faded glory, one that is slowly but inexorably vanishing, rather than a world that is coming into being.

In a way, the Church is like well-known companies such as Sears or McDonald's that have been around seemingly forever. Everyone knows — or thinks they know — what those companies and ours (the Catholic Church) are all about. But at least in the case of the Church, they are wrong; they really don't have a clue, and part of the reason they don't have a clue is *my* fault. It may be yours, too, by the way.

I've heard countless stories over the years of Catholics just going through the motions — of not even trying to sing hymns, of not grasping the most basic tenets of their faith, and of not even caring about their own lack of knowledge. Many of these tales are true, or at least true enough. But who is at fault for this? Who is responsible? Aren't I at fault when I don't even glance at the hymnal as the organ is playing and the cantor is desperately trying to get the congregation to produce a noise that could at least pass for vocal music? Aren't I at fault when I approach the altar to receive the body of Christ in exactly the way I approach a fast-food counter to order a hamburger and a Coke? What message do those things send to the non-Catholic, the potential but undecided convert? For that matter, what message does it send to our children?

The average non-Catholic who attends a Catholic Mass may not be impressed by anything except the lethargy of the congregation and the mechanical approach to sacred things.

And for this, I am at fault.

Imagine the potential convert who musters up the courage — it takes more than you think — to enter a Catholic church for the first time. In place of warmth and welcome that person is likely to find an indifference which will be interpreted as coldness. That potential convert is also likely to see people leaving church right after Holy Communion without even a moment's reflection. What is she to make of that after reading of the Church's teaching concerning the Real Presence? What about the virtual stampede for the door before the first notes of the recessional hymn are played?

Can you imagine what these things make a potential convert think? I can because I experienced them all. I imagine there are many potential converts who showed up once in a Catholic church and then never again because of things exactly like this. The potential convert is looking for signs that he's on the right trail. These are not those signs — just the opposite, in fact. Becoming Catholic can take more perseverance than you think.

And for this, I am at fault.

I will never forget my dad's advice: "Look for a church where people are allowing themselves to be transformed by the Gospel."

Do I really see that transformation in my parish? Do you really see it in yours? St. Paul writes the following: "So whoever is in Christ is a new creation: the old things have passed away; behold, new things have come" (2 Corinthians 5:17). Are we really new creations, or are we still mired in the old, the things that should have passed away — that *would* have passed away if we had taken our conversions seriously enough, if we had cooperated with God's grace and permitted the sacraments to do their work in us.

But I have not done these things, and for this I am at fault.

I sometimes look around at Mass and wonder if there's any evidence of transformation, of conversion. I might see a woman who is a pathological gossip, another who publicly and loudly espouses views on abortion that are completely at odds with Church teaching, a man who is brutally critical of the priest, another who drinks to excess at the expense of his family. Where is the transformation?

Then, I catch myself and feel my cheeks redden. What am I doing looking around at Mass in the first place? Why isn't my attention focused on the altar? What right have I to criticize anyone? I need the Sacrament of Reconciliation as much as anyone and more than most. So instead, I force myself to look inward and marvel at my own intransigence — how my conversion seems to be put on hold far more often than it should be. Even with all the advantages anyone could ask for — the sacraments, Tradition, the Magisterium, the Communion of Saints, sacred Scripture, you name it — I recognize that my own transformation is far from complete. Much more radical change is necessary.

And when I think these thoughts, I become aware that I have become a stumbling block to others, and I am saddened.

So what do we do to overcome the Church's branding problem? How do we stop becoming stumbling blocks?

We simply walk again the path of conversion. We turn again to the only source of transformation — of life — that there is. We turn to the Christ who is revealed to us in the Church's sacramental life. We allow Him to feed us, to nourish us, to support us. We allow Him to knock us out of our doldrums (He's actually very good at that). And then we have a chance of becoming that "new creation" of which St. Paul speaks. That's why my sadness is always temporary. Christ is there in His sacraments and His Church to turn sadness, weakness, and sinfulness into joy and hope.

Yes, the Church has a branding problem, but it's a problem that could be fixed. All it takes is a few million conversions. So why not make yours one of the first?

If you could do that and I could do it too, the Church would be given new life, a new springtime. Our lives would be transformed. We would no longer be stumbling blocks. We would actually become the people we were created to be.

All things considered, that's not a bad deal. You see, despite my own hardheadedness, my life has been transformed in the most incredible ways. I have repented, and have been forgiven. I have been drawn closer to Jesus Christ more than I could have ever imagined by way of the Catholic Church and her sacraments. My work, my relationships, and even my struggles have been sanctified. I *love* being Catholic.

So don't let me — or any of the other stumbling blocks that stand in your way — stop you. I invite you to join me, and to allow yourself to be completely transformed by Christ in His Catholic Church. You'll be eternally grateful you did.

Acknowledgments

I am eternally grateful to my wife, Kathi, my companion on this journey of faith and life, and to our children Christian (and his wife, Erin), T.J. (and his wife, Kayla), Sarah (and her husband, Kyle), Daniel, Maria, Joseph, David, and Hannah. You have all been an indescribably important part of my life, and I love you all more than words can express.

Speaking of faith and life, both are precious gifts for which I have my parents, Douglas and Margaret Lowry, to thank. Dad has encouraged, inspired, and put up with me by way of heroic virtue, and Mom has served as a shining example of service, enthusiasm, and caring throughout my life (some of her friends refer to her as St. Margaret of Steubenville). As my dear late friend Father Ray Ryland observed, I did a great job picking my parents. I couldn't agree more.

There have also been countless good friends along the way who have contributed to my ongoing conversion, perhaps none so much as my longtime friend and former boss Marcus Grodi and the staff of The Coming Home Network International. Thank you. Likewise, my association with Our Sunday Visitor as a reader, writer, and board member has been a privilege. Ditto the Columbus chapter of Legatus. It would also be difficult to overstate my debt of gratitude to the many wonderful people at Franciscan University of Steubenville.

Finally, so many individuals: Mike Aquilina, Randy Hain, Dan Burke, Michael Warsaw, Donna-Marie Cooper O'Boyle, Tom Peterson, Andreas Widmer, Teresa Tomeo, Jennifer Fulwiler, Andy and Myrna Molinari, Bob Geiger, Brian Patrick, Devin Rose, Scott and Kimberly Hahn,

Pat Madrid, Paul Thigpen, Steve Ray, Billy Newton, Gary Zimack, Mike McCartney, Father John Riccardo, Father Thomas Blau, Father Rocky Hoffman, Mike Hernon, Don Brey, Kevin Knight, Sister Theresa Aletheia Noble, Rachel Muha, Don Materniak, Don Kissinger, Jim Harold, Regis Martin, Monsignor Frank Lane, Father Kevin Lutz, Father Stash Dailey, the Wakely family, Mike D'Andrea, Mary Ann Jepsen, Marian Schuda, John Gioffre, Tim and Mary Ellen Jakubisin, Bob Doelling, Tom Blee, Father Al McBride, Father Val Peter, Bishop Kevin Rhoades, Bishop Robert Baker, Albino and Joyce Aragno, Ernie and Pat Fletcher, Ed and Loretta Maher, Steve and Eileen Dluzynski, Jim and Benerada Wahlberg, Greg Erlandson, Kyle Hamilton, Linda Teeters, Andy and Julie Naporano, Mark Shea, Kevin Vost, Shane Kapler, Annie Egan, Matt Swaim, Sarah Reinhard, Patrick Novecosky, Bill Messerly, Dave Orsborn, Marc Hawk, Roy Lydic, Will Turek, Mike Parker, Gary Irvine, Rob Rissmeyer, Dick Kurth, Tom Caldwell, Dan Spencer, Mark Middendorf, Chris Stefanick, Pat Lencioni, Keith Borchers, Bob and Beth Tatz, Bill and Theresa Warren, Dave Geenens, Brother Rex Anthony Norris, Cindy Cavnar, Jill Adamson, George Foster, Jeff Rayis, Joe Patrick, Ed Rivalsky, Jon and Carol Forrest, Chuck and Jo Ann Wilson, Mary Lou Gorno, Ruth Hanlin and all my favorite aunts — and last but certainly not least, my most excellent collaborator on this project, John Collins.

Thank you!

MAY 2017